Algebra

Chad Troutwine · Markus Moberg · Chris Kane · Mark Glenn

Co-Founders	Chad Troutwine
	Markus Moberg
Managing Editor	Mark Glenn
Director of Academic Programs	Brian Galvin
Interior Design	Miriam Lubow
	Lisa Johnson
Cover Design	Nick Mason
	Mike Miller
Contributing Editors	Megan Kucik
	Tatiana Becker
	Marisa Peck
Contributing Writers	Jason Cauthen
	Ryan Licwinko

A successful educational program is only as good as the people who teach it, and Veritas Prep is fortunate to have many of the world's finest GMAT instructors on its team.

Not only does that team know how to teach a strong curriculum, but it also knows how to help create one. This lesson book would not be possible without the hundreds of suggestions we have received from our talented faculty all across the world– from Seattle, Detroit, and Miami to London, Singapore, and Dubai. Their passion for excellence helped give birth to a new curriculum that is far better than what we could have created on our own.

Our students also deserve a very special thanks. Thousands of them have provided us with something priceless: enthusiastic feedback that has guided us in creating the most comprehensive GMAT preparation course available on the market today.

We therefore dedicate this revised lesson book to all Veritas Prep instructors and students who have tackled the GMAT and given us their valuable input along the way.

Table of Contents

Introduction 1

Lesson

Algebra 2
Exponents 3
Roots 10
Algebraic Number Properties.. 13
Algebraic Calculations and Factoring 16
Algebraic Equations 19
Inequalities 28
Functions 34

Assorted Problems

Function Applications 36
Algebraic Word Problems 37
Exponents and Roots 56
Algebraic Calculations 70
Algebraic Number Properties 85
Common Algebraic Equations 101
Inequalities 107
Function Questions 117

Solutions

Lesson Problems 120
Assorted Problems 123

Answer Key 150

Lesson 4 Introduction

Algebra is a key skill on the GMAT, yet there is no Quantitative topic that strikes more fear into the hearts of test takers. Beginning with mastery of the fundamentals, covered in the Math Essentials lesson, the Veritas Prep course encompasses all of the Algebra concepts tested by the GMAT. The Veritas Prep strategies in this lesson build on those fundamentals to give you the insight you need to tackle every Algebra problem confidently and efficiently.

Algebra

Algebra

Algebra problems make up approximately 25% of the Quantitative portion on the GMAT. As in the Arithmetic lesson, we will break down Algebra into all the possible question types that exist on the GMAT and provide detailed approaches to all these different types.

On the GMAT, your knowledge of Algebra can be tested in numerous ways. The standard problems ask you to solve for one or more unknowns, usually in the form of word problems. Often, however, you are not providing a solution to a problem but rather manipulating an equation so that you can recognize an equivalent form. On other questions you are working strictly with roots and exponents. Regardless of the question type, most Algebra problems test your knowledge of a finite set of rules as well as your ability to solve for unknowns or recognize equivalent forms of an equation.

Exponents

Mastering the rules and question types associated with exponents is an essential skill for tackling Algebra problems on the GMAT. In the Math Basics lesson, you were given a basic introduction to the rules for exponents. In this section, we are going to expand upon those rules and show how exponents are tested on the GMAT.

Exponent Rules

Before we look at 5 important rules for working with exponents, let's review some definitions:

x^n means x to the nth power, or x multiplied by itself n times.

$x \cdot x \cdot x \cdot x \cdot x = x^5$

$32 = 2 \cdot 2 \cdot 2 \cdot 2 \cdot 2 = 2^5$

$x^1 = x$

$x^0 = 1$ (for $x \neq 0$)

$x^{-a} = \dfrac{1}{x^a}$ (for $x \neq 0$)   *Example:* $2^{-2} = \dfrac{1}{2^2} = \dfrac{1}{4}$

$\dfrac{1}{x^{-a}} = x^a$ (for $x \neq 0$)   *Example:* $\dfrac{1}{3^{-3}} = \dfrac{3^3}{1} = 3^3 = 27$

In the following pages we will examine 5 important rules for working with exponents along with several examples and sample questions:

I. $x^a \cdot x^b = x^{a+b}$ *Example:* $3^2 \cdot 3^3 = 3^5$

When you are multiplying numbers or variables with like bases, add the exponents. You can only add exponents when the bases are identical.

$$y^a \cdot x^b \neq (xy)^{a+b}$$

Let's look at a more difficult example of this rule: *What is $x \cdot x^a \cdot x^a$?*

Answer

Don't forget that any variable without a given exponent really has an exponent of 1. For instance $x = x^1$. In this problem, you add $1 + a + a$ so the result is x^{2a+1}.

> *How Your Mind Works:* Do not forget to include the understood exponent of 1 in exponent calculations with variables. This is a very common error on exponent questions.

II. $\dfrac{x^a}{x^b} = x^{a-b}$ (for $x \neq 0$)   *Example:* $\dfrac{4^{10}}{4^7} = 4^3$

When you are dividing variables or numbers with like bases, subtract the exponents. You can only subtract exponents if the bases are the same.

Note

This rule is really the same as the first rule because another way to write $\dfrac{x^a}{x^b} = x^{a-b}$ is simply $x^a \cdot x^{-b} = x^{a+(-b)} = x^{a-b}$

As with multiplication, don't forget that $x = x^1$ *Example:* $\dfrac{x}{x^a} = x^{1-a}$

III. $(x^a)^b = x^{a \cdot b}$ *Example:* $(7^3)^8 = 7^{24}$

When you are raising a variable with an exponent to another power, multiply the exponents. Note that the location of the parentheses is very important:

$$x^{(3)^2} = x^9 \text{ not } x^6$$

Let's look at an example that combines the first several rules:

$$4^4 \cdot 2^3 \cdot 8^2 = ?$$

As the equation stands, we are not allowed to combine exponents because we do not have like bases. However, by recognizing that these are all powers of 2, we can create like bases. Since $4 = 2^2$ and $8 = 2^3$, the equation now looks like this:

$$(2^2)^4 \cdot 2^3 \cdot (2^3)^2$$

Using the third exponent rule, we can remove all parentheses and then add exponents because of like bases:

$$2^8 \cdot 2^3 \cdot 2^6 = 2^{(8 + 3 + 6)} = 2^{17}$$

Once you have mastered these three important rules, you still must be prepared for difficult and unusual questions. Let's look at a moderate GMAT question that tests your understanding of these first three exponent rules:

1.   If $27^{2x + 4} = 3^{3x + 9}$, then $x =$

Think Like the Test Maker: The GMAT likes to test your knowledge of exponent rules, and one way to make a problem more difficult is to test several exponent rules in a single question.

(A)   -3

(B)   -1

(C)   0

(D)   1

(E)   3

Note

GMAC could have made the problem easier simply by removing one of the steps/exponent rules involved:

If $3^{6x + 12} = 3^{3x + 9}$, then $x =$

(A)   -3

(B)   -1

(C)   0

(D)   1

(E)   3

IV. $(x \cdot y)^a = x^a \cdot y^a$ **Example**: $(3 \cdot 4)^2 = 3^2 \cdot 4^2$

When the product of variables or numbers is raised to a certain power, you can distribute the exponent among each number or variable. Using the example above, do not forget that if the given number can be factored, the same rule applies:

$12^2 = (3 \cdot 4)^2 = 3^2 \cdot 4^2 = 144$

> **GMAT Insider**: Do not forget that you can factor numbers and distribute the exponents. This is an important skill on many exponent questions.

For division the rule is the same:

V. $\left(\dfrac{x}{y}\right)^a = \left(\dfrac{x^a}{y^a}\right)$ **Example**: $\left(\dfrac{2}{3}\right)^4 = \dfrac{2^4}{3^4} = \dfrac{16}{81}$

When any fraction is raised to a certain power, you can distribute the exponent to each number or variable in that fraction.

Factoring and Exponents

An essential skill for all exponent questions is to manipulate each side of an equation using the preceding exponent rules in order to make the two sides of an equation look identical. Consider this simple example:

$4^3 = 2^x$

In order to find a value for x, we must first manipulate the left side of the equation so that the bases are identical. Then, we can see that $2^6 = 2^x$ and $x = 6$. This approach does not change when we have multiple bases and multiple variables. Consider the following example:

$2^x \cdot 3^y \cdot 5^z = 2^5 \cdot 3^4 \cdot 5^5$

The important question is this: Now that we are dealing with multiple bases and multiple variables, are we still able to determine the value of x, y, and z?

The answer is yes. Why?

Because if each side of the equation has identical prime bases, then the exponents must equal one another, no matter how many distinct numbers there are.

Detailed Explanation:

Because 2, 3, and 5 are prime numbers, the only way this equation can be true is if the exponents on each side are the same. This type of problem tests your fundamental understanding of factors – in other words, you must realize that no matter how many 2s you have on one side, those 2s can never combine with other numbers to result in a 5 or a 3 and vice versa. Because this property of numbers is true, your goal in exponent questions is always to make each side of the equation contain the same prime numbers and then equate the exponents.

Let's look at a classic exponent problem that tests all the rules and question types we have learned thus far:

2.   If x and y are positive integers and $75^y 27^{2y+1} = 5^4 3^x$, what is the value of x?

(A)   8

(B)   10

(C)   12

(D)   15

(E)   17

Addition and Subtraction with Exponents

The rules that we learned in the previous section apply to all forms of multiplication and division with exponents. When dealing with addition and subtraction of terms containing exponents, however, there are no specific exponent rules. Instead, you must rely on your understanding of factoring and combining like terms. Let's look at an example.

3. $2^{4x} + 2^{4x} + 2^{4x} + 2^{4x} = 4^{24}$. What is x?

(A)   3

(B)   5

(C)   6

(D)   8.5

(E)   11.5

Here is one more difficult example of addition and subtraction of exponents: $3^5 + 3^8 - 3^7 - 3^6 = ?$

Factor out 3^5: $3^5(1 + 3^3 - 3^2 - 3) = 3^5(1 + 27 - 9 - 3) = 16(3^5)$

GMAT Insider: Whenever you have multiplication or division of numbers or variables with exponents, use the exponent rules listed in this section. However, with addition and subtraction of exponents rely on your understanding of factoring to combine like terms and then use any necessary exponent rules. Addition and subtraction of exponents and roots is the most common area of difficulty for students in this section and should be thoroughly understood before taking the test.

Common Exponents

Exponent calculations can be made more quickly when you have basic powers memorized:

$(-1)^2 = 1$

$0^2 = 0$

$1^2 = 1$

$2^2 = 4$	$2^3 = 8$	$2^4 = 16$	$2^5 = 32$	$2^6 = 64$
$3^2 = 9$	$3^3 = 27$	$3^4 = 81$		
$4^2 = 16$	$4^3 = 64$	$4^4 = 256$		
$5^2 = 25$	$5^3 = 125$	$5^4 = 625$		
$6^2 = 36$	$7^2 = 49$	$8^2 = 64$	$9^2 = 81$	$10^2 = 100$
$11^2 = 121$	$12^2 = 144$	$13^2 = 169$	$14^2 = 196$	$15^2 = 225$

How Your Mind Works: $25^2 = 625$, not 225! This is a common student mistake.

Algebra

Roots

Because all roots can be expressed as exponents, the rules governing roots are the same for exponents. Still, there are subtle differences in how to approach root problems on the GMAT and it is important that students recognize these. First let's refresh how to express roots with both radicals and exponents:

Any value for a in the root $\sqrt[a]{x}$ is possible. This simply means that we are looking for the number that when raised to the power of a equals x.

We will be learning more about the positive and negative number properties of roots and exponents in the next section. Let's first look at some examples and rules relating to different roots:

$$(\sqrt[4]{25})^2 = (25^{\frac{1}{4}})^2 = 25^{\left(\frac{1}{4}\right) \cdot 2} = 25^{\frac{2}{4}} = 25^{\frac{1}{2}} = \sqrt{25} = 5$$

Note

$\sqrt[4]{25^2} = (\sqrt[4]{25})^2$ because the order of operations is not important in determining the answer. You can square 25 first and then find the 4th root, or you can find the 4th root first and then square that number.

Consider the following examples:

A. *What is $\sqrt[\frac{1}{2}]{8}$?*

B. *What is $64^{\frac{2}{3}}$?*

Facts & Formulas: $\sqrt[a]{x}$ can be rewritten as $x^{\frac{1}{a}}$. The square root $\sqrt{x}$ is the same as $\sqrt[2]{x}$. There are two square roots for every positive number x, but when the radical sign is written out as in this example: "What is the $\sqrt{16}$?" then the question is asking for the principal (positive) square root only. To emphasize: The two square roots of 16 are +4 and -4 but $\sqrt{16}$ is equal to positive 4 only.

Answers:

A. $\sqrt[\frac{1}{2}]{8} = 8^2 = 64$

B. $64^{\frac{2}{3}} = (\sqrt[3]{64})^2 = 4^2 = 16$

Let's look at basic rules for combining and factorizing roots:

Definitions for Factorizing Roots

As long as the roots are the same (all square root or third root, etc.) then these rules apply. The examples are given with square roots, but they can be replaced with any roots.

I. $\sqrt{\dfrac{a}{b}} = \dfrac{\sqrt{a}}{\sqrt{b}}$　　　　$\sqrt{\dfrac{1}{16}} = \dfrac{\sqrt{1}}{\sqrt{16}} = \dfrac{1}{4}$ and $\sqrt{\dfrac{7}{16}} = \dfrac{\sqrt{7}}{\sqrt{16}} = \dfrac{\sqrt{7}}{4}$

II. $\sqrt{a \cdot b} = \sqrt{a} \cdot \sqrt{b}$　　　　$\sqrt{72} = \sqrt{36 \cdot 2} = \sqrt{36} \cdot \sqrt{2} = 6\sqrt{2}$ and
$\sqrt{3} \cdot \sqrt{12} = \sqrt{3 \cdot 12} = \sqrt{36} = 6$

In other unusual roots it is advisable to first change to exponent form, use the exponent rules, and then make the necessary calculations. Otherwise, leave roots in the form as shown above .

Addition and Subtraction of Roots

GMAT Insider: While unusual roots are possible on the GMAT, most questions deal with the square roots of numbers.

Add and subtract roots as you learned with exponents:

$x + x + x + x = 4x$　　$\sqrt{2} + \sqrt{2} + \sqrt{2} + \sqrt{2} = 4\sqrt{2}$

($4\sqrt{2}$ is the same as $4 \cdot \sqrt{2}$)

Algebra

As with variables, you can only combine like roots.

$x + x + y = 2x + y$ $\sqrt{2} + \sqrt{2} + \sqrt{8} = 2\sqrt{2} + \sqrt{8}$

However, remember what you learned about factorizing roots:

$\sqrt{2} + \sqrt{2} + \sqrt{8} = 2\sqrt{2} + \sqrt{8} = 2\sqrt{2} + \sqrt{4 \cdot 2} = 2\sqrt{2} + \sqrt{4}\sqrt{2} = 2\sqrt{2} + 2\sqrt{2} = 4\sqrt{2}$

Note
$\sqrt{12} + \sqrt{4} \neq \sqrt{16}$
As with exponents, you are not allowed to combine unlike terms.

Note
It is not standard form to have roots in the denominator. Consider the expression $\frac{9}{\sqrt{3}}$

To remove the root from the denominator multiply the expression by $\frac{\sqrt{3}}{\sqrt{3}}$

After that manipulation, you are left with $\frac{9}{\sqrt{3}}\left(\frac{\sqrt{3}}{\sqrt{3}}\right) = \frac{9\sqrt{3}}{3} = 3\sqrt{3}$

Another way to think about this is: $\frac{3^2}{3^{\frac{1}{2}}} = 3^{\frac{3}{2}} = 3^1 \cdot 3^{\frac{1}{2}} = 3\sqrt{3}$

> **Facts & Formulas:** Students should memorize that $\sqrt{8} = 2\sqrt{2}$ and that $\sqrt{27} = 3\sqrt{3}$

4.   What is $\sqrt{98} + \sqrt{32} + \sqrt{8}$?

(A) $6\sqrt{8}$

(B) $7\sqrt{8}$

(C) $8\sqrt{2}$

(D) $13\sqrt{2}$

(E) $14\sqrt{2}$

Algebraic Number Properties

In addition to the number properties that we learned in the Arithmetic lesson, there are several important attributes of numbers that relate specifically to the Algebra material. Most of these relate to exponents and roots.

Exponent Number Properties

I. Any number or variable raised to an even exponent will always be positive or zero.

Examples: x^2, $(-4)^6$, y^{20} $(5-x)^4$

II. When a variable is raised to an even exponent, we know the result is positive or zero but we do not know the sign of the variable.

Examples: If $x^2 = 4$, then $x = 2$ or -2 (two solutions)
  If $(5 - x)^4 = 81$, then $x = 2$ or 8 (two solutions)
  If $x^2 = 0$, then $x = 0$ (one solution)
  If $x^2 = -1$, then there is no real solution (i.e., $x^2 = -1$ cannot be true on the GMAT)

III. When a number or variable is raised to an odd exponent, the result can be positive, negative, or zero.

Examples: x^3, y^5, or x^{27} can be either $+$ or $-$ (or 0)
  $(-4)^3 = -64$
  $5^3 = 125$

IV. When a variable is raised to an odd exponent, the sign of the result determines the sign of the variable, and there will always be one solution.

Examples: If $x^3 = -125$ then $x = -5$ and if $x^3 = 64$ then x is $+4$

V. When a number between 0 and 1 is squared, the result becomes smaller. For all other real numbers greater than 1 or less than 0, the square of that number becomes greater.

Examples: $\left(\frac{1}{2}\right)^2 = \frac{1}{4}$ $\qquad$ $(.4)^2 = .16$ $\qquad$ $-(.4)^2 = -(.16)$ $\qquad$ $(-.4)^2 = .16$

Let's look at a couple of GMAT problems that test these number properties:

5. $\quad$ Is $xy < 0$?

$\qquad$ (1) $\qquad$ $x^2y^3 < 0$

$\qquad$ (2) $\qquad$ $xy^2 > 0$

(A) $\qquad$ Statement (1) ALONE is sufficient, but statement (2) alone is not sufficient.

(B) $\qquad$ Statement (2) ALONE is sufficient, but statement (1) alone is not sufficient.

(C) $\qquad$ BOTH statements TOGETHER are sufficient, but NEITHER statement ALONE is sufficient.

(D) $\qquad$ EACH statement ALONE is sufficient.

(E) $\qquad$ Statements (1) and (2) TOGETHER are NOT sufficient.

6. $\quad$ If $x^2 < x$, which of the following could be a value of x?

(A) $\qquad$ - 6

(B) $\qquad$ $-\frac{2}{3}$

(C) $\qquad$ $\frac{6}{7}$

(D) $\qquad$ $\frac{5}{4}$

(E) $\qquad$ 25

Unit's Digit Properties with Exponents

Just as we learned that there is a distinct pattern for determining the unit's digit for any products, this is also true with exponents. In the following chart, the vertical row represents the exponent and the horizontal row represents the unit's digit for any number. By looking at the chart you can see that there is a repeating pattern for all units' digits raised to a certain power. In other words, it is possible to determine the unit's digit of a huge number $(1,234,678)^{23}$ very quickly because such a pattern exists. Look at the chart for any number ending in 8 and see that risen to the 1st power the units digit will be 6, and then the pattern repeats itself. Because the cycle repeats every 4th exponent you know that the unit's digit for $(1,234,678)^{23}$ is the same as the unit's digit for $(8)^3$ which is 2. Again, you do not need to memorize this table, just know that it exists.

		Unit's Digit							
		1	2	3	4	5	6	7	8	9
Exponent	1	1	2	3	4	5	6	7	8	9
	2	1	4	9	6	5	6	9	4	1
	3	1	8	7	4	5	6	3	2	9
	4	1	6	1	6	5	6	1	6	1
	5	1	2	3	4	5	6	7	8	9
	6	1	4	9	6	5	6	9	4	1
	7	1	8	7	4	5	6	3	2	9
	8	1	6	1	6	5	6	1	6	1
	9	1	2	3	4	5	6	7	8	9

Facts & Formulas: $\sqrt{16}$ = positive 4 only, but when $x^2 = 16$, then $x = +4$ and -4 .

$\sqrt{-16}$ is not a real number so there is no solution on the GMAT for this calculation.

Root Number Properties

I. For even roots of all positive numbers, there are two solutions – one positive and one negative. However, when the radical sign is used, the question is only asking for the principal square root. There is only one solution for an even root of 0, and the even root of a negative number is not a real number, so there is no solution on the GMAT.

II. For odd roots of all real numbers, there is exactly one solution which can be negative, positive, or 0. *Examples*: $\sqrt[3]{-27} = -3$ $\sqrt[5]{32} = 2$ $\sqrt[3]{0} = 0$

III. When taking the square root of a number between 0 and 1, the result is greater than the original number. For all positive numbers greater than 1, the square root of that number will be less than the original number.

Examples: $\sqrt{\frac{1}{4}} = \frac{1}{2}$ $\sqrt{25} = 5$

Algebraic Calculations and Factoring

On the GMAT, you must be very comfortable working with algebraic equations. To do this effectively, you must have a strong command of the rules governing algebraic calculations. These rules involve factoring, simplifying, combining like terms, etc. We have dealt with many of the necessary rules in the Math Essentials lesson and in the Exponents and Roots section. Let's examine a few of those important rules more closely:

Order of Operations

The order in which to carry out calculations in an algebraic equation is crucial. For instance, $2 \cdot 3 + 4$ could be incorrectly interpreted as $2(3 + 4)$. When solving an algebraic equation, carry out the calculations in this order:

1. **P**arentheses
2. **E**xponents
3. **M**ultiplications
4. **D**ivisions
5. **A**dditions
6. **S**ubtractions

> *Habits of Great Test Takers:* One key to my test-taking success lies in making common test concepts a part of my lifestyle. I read academic articles, solve math puzzles, listen to competing arguments, and debate issues. I make a habit of asking "why?" and "how?" I play number and logic games, perform thought exercises, and think critically when reading the news. And most importantly, I approach each problem as a challenge of my ability to "get it." Turning a "chore" into a "challenge" not only made studying more enjoyable, but helped lift my score into the top tier!
> – Joseph Dise, Paris

The mnemonic device to remember this order is: **P**lease **E**xcuse **M**y **D**ear **A**unt **S**ally

What is $\frac{1}{2} + \frac{3}{2} \cdot \frac{3}{2} \div \frac{9}{4} - \frac{1}{2}$?

Answer
Following the proper order of operations, the answer is 1.

Parentheses

Dealing with parentheses in algebraic calculations can result in many careless errors. Be very careful in these calculations and follow the proper rules.

To multiply an algebraic expression in parentheses with a number or a variable, multiply every term within the parentheses by the number or the variable.

$a(b + c) = ab + ac$

To multiply two algebraic expressions with each other, multiply every term in one set of parentheses with every term in the other set of parentheses.

$(a + b)(c + d) = ac + ad + bc + bd$

As you may remember, this type of calculation can be accomplished using the **FOIL** shortcut for distributing the multiplication
(**F**irst **O**utside **I**nside **L**ast).

Example: $2\left(\dfrac{20x}{11}\right) = 3(x+7)$ *Solve for x.*

Remove parentheses so that the equation looks as follows: $\dfrac{40x}{11} = 3x + 21$

Remove the denominator on the left side of the equation by multiplying both sides of the

equation by 11: $40x = 33x + 21(11)$

Note
Do not multiply out 21(11) as it is easier to work within its factored form.

Combine like terms on each side of the = sign: $7x = 21(11)$
Divide both sides by 7 and solve for $x = 33$.

> ***Lazy Genius***: Always avoid unnecessary multiplication if the number is going to be divided again later.

> ***GMAT Insider***: Being comfortable and efficient with algebraic calculations is an essential skill on the GMAT. It is also a weakness for many students who have embedded "algebra flaws" in the way they carry out calculations. If you are struggling to solve algebraic equations quickly, show your instructor some of the problems you are having so that she can help you eliminate the flaws.

Algebra

Algebraic Factoring

All of the rules we used previously for expanding parentheses can be used in reverse. On many GMAT problems you have to recognize this fact and pull out common factors to form parentheses. We addressed the skill in the Exponents and Roots section but let's look at it in a few different contexts. Let's start with an easier GMAT problem testing factoring:

7. $\dfrac{5 + 5\sqrt{5}}{10 + \sqrt{500}} =$

(A) $\dfrac{1}{2}$

(B)   2

(C) $1 + \sqrt{5}$

(D) $1 + 5\sqrt{5}$

(E) $5 + \sqrt{5}$

After we examine some of the common algebraic equations, we will apply the important concept of factoring to a variety of different problems and drills.

Algebraic Equations

Now that we have reviewed the rules for working with algebraic expressions, let's look at some common equation types. The most common algebraic equations on the GMAT are linear equations with one, two, or three unknowns. A linear equation means that all variables have an exponent of one[1].

Linear Equations with One Variable

Dealing with a one variable equation is generally straightforward. Get the variable by itself by performing a series of operations (addition, subtraction, multiplication, and division). Always perform the same operation on both sides of the equation.

However, as we learned in the previous section, these equations can sometimes involve difficult algebraic calculation rules. To solve for one variable, use the rules learned previously and solve for the unknown:

Example: *Solve for x.* $x \cdot 4 + 7 = 15$

Using your PEMDAS rules, first multiply x times 4 to get $4x + 7 = 15$. Combine like terms to get $4x = 8$ and divide by 4 so that $x = 2$.

[1] Technically, it means that when graphed in the coordinate geometry plane, it will create a straight line – thus the term *linear*.

Algebra

Linear Equations with Multiple Variables

Most GMAT problems require more than one variable. When solving a problem with *n* variables, you generally need *n* different equations to solve for all the variables.

Note

While it is usually true that you need *n* different equations to solve for *n* different variables, it is sometimes possible to solve for multiple variables with fewer equations (exponent problems, small set problems, etc.). We will examine these unique question types in more detail in the Data Sufficiency lesson.

The substitution approach to equations with multiple unknowns:

1.   Express one variable using the other variables in an equation.

2.   Plug this new expression into another of the given equations.

3.   Repeat until you solve one variable, and then substitute the variable with its value in the other equations.

Example: $x + y = 7$
$x - y = 1$ *(two equations and two unknowns, x and y)*

> *GMAT Insider:* On the GMAT, most equations you need to solve will involve two unknowns. While you must occasionally deal with three unknowns, it is highly unlikely that you will encounter more than three unknowns and three equations. Data Sufficiency problems may present four equations and four unknowns, but you won't need to *solve* them.

Express one variable using the other variables in an equation.

$x - y = 1 \rightarrow x = 1 + y$

Plug this new expression into another of the given equations.

$x + y = 7 \rightarrow (1 + y) + y = 7 \rightarrow 2y = 7 - 1 \rightarrow y = 3$

Repeat until you solve one variable, and then substitute the variable with its value in the other equations.

$x = 1 + y \rightarrow x = 1 + 3 \rightarrow x = 4$

You can start with either variable and with either equation. Note that by starting with x, you solve for y first. Solving by substitution will always work and must be thoroughly understood by students. However, it is generally faster to solve equations directly by adding or subtracting to eliminate terms. Most problems on the GMAT should be solved using this approach – that is, by solving simultaneously.

Solving Simultaneously

Add or subtract both sides of two or more equations to solve the equation directly.

Example: $x + y = 7$

$x - y = 1$ *(two equations and two unknowns, x and y)*

Add both sides of the two equations together.

$(x + y) + (x - y) = 7 + 1 \rightarrow 2x = 8 \rightarrow x = 4$

In either equation, substitute one of the variables with its known value.

$x + y = 7 \rightarrow 4 + y = 7 \rightarrow y = 3$

Let's look at a few examples of solving for multiple variables using the two different approaches:

Example: *2x - y = -5 and x + 2y = 20. Solve for x.*

Solution
Arrange the equations on top of each other with like terms in line.
$2x - y = -5$
$x + 2y = 20$

Since our goal is to eliminate y, multiply the top equation by 2 and then combine.

$$4x - 2y = -10$$
$$\underline{+ (x + 2y = 20)}$$
$$5x = 10$$
$$x = 2$$

Similarly, since we know immediately that $y = 2x + 5$, substitution is equally fast in this example. Substitute for y in the 2nd equation and $x + 2(2x + 5) = 20$.

Remove the parentheses and $x + 4x + 10 = 20 \rightarrow 5x = 10 \rightarrow x = 2$.

> *Lazy Genius*: Which Method?
> Approach any multi-variable problem expecting to use only the substitution approach. However, you can save time if you see that variables from different equations will cancel each other out when two or more equations are added or subtracted. Generally speaking, use the substitution approach when it is not easy to cancel out terms but use the direct approach on all other problems.

When dealing with 3 unknowns, substitution is time-consuming and tedious. Always try to solve simultaneously by putting two of the three equations together to eliminate variables. Let's look at a good example with three unknowns:

Example:
$x + y + z = 0$
$x - y - z = 6$ (three equations and three unknowns, x, y, and z)
$x + y - z = 20$

First use the alternative approach and then substitute.

$(x + y + z) + (x - y - z) = 0 + 6 \rightarrow 2x = 6 \rightarrow x = 3$

$(3 + y + z) + (3 + y - z) = 0 + 20 \rightarrow 6 + 2y = 20 \rightarrow y = 7$

$3 + 7 + z = 0 \rightarrow z = -10$

Quadratic Equations

A quadratic equation is an equation that contains a squared variable. Unlike linear equations, quadratic equations cannot be solved simply by combining like terms and isolating the unknown. Specifically, a quadratic equation is an equation in the form:

$ax^2 + bx + c = 0$ (where a, b, and c are numbers of any value, including 0)

Example: $x^2 + 2x = 24$

To solve this equation, it is necessary to first put the equation in the form listed above. We do this by moving the 24 to the left side of the equation to get $x^2 + 2x - 24 = 0$. Now we factor "by inspection" because this is an easily factored quadratic. To factor by inspection, we find the set of factors of 24 that when added or subtracted will give us positive 2. That set is 6 and 4. The larger number will need to be positive and the smaller number negative. The quadratic can be rewritten as $(x + 6)(x - 4) = 0$ and the solutions are now clear as $x = -6$ and 4.

For the quadratic $x^2 + 2x - 24 = 0$ the roots or factors are defined as $(x + 6)$ and $(x - 4)$ and the solutions are defined as $x = -6$ and 4.

Algebra

An alternative to factoring by inspection is using the Quadratic Formula:

For the equation $ax^2 + bx + c = 0$, $x = \dfrac{-b \pm \sqrt{b^2 - 4ac}}{2a}$

As the formula indicates, there are normally two solutions to x in an equation involving x^2.

The exceptions are: If $b^2 - 4ac = 0$, then there is only one solution.
If $b^2 - 4ac < 0$, then there are no solutions.

Note
Only use the formula for an equation involving one squared variable.

When faced with a quadratic equation on the GMAT, you have three options to solve it:

1. <u>Factoring by inspection</u> is the best option if you can do it quickly.

2. <u>Plugging in</u> the answer choices is often useful.

3. <u>Using the quadratic formula</u> is always an option, but remember:
    If it gets messy you can probably solve it quicker by factoring or plugging in!

Example: $3y^2 + 5y + 2 = 0$ $(a = 3, b = 5, c = 2)$

It is possible to solve this quadratic by factoring. To do this, first create the left side of your two roots by breaking down 3 into its two factors: 1 and 3. Because 2 is also prime, there is only one set of factors we can use for it: 2 and 1. The only question is where to put the 2 and 1, and by inspection you can see that the 1 must be multiplied by the 3 and the 2 by the 1.

$(3y + 2)(y + 1) = 0$

$y = \dfrac{-2}{3}$ and -1

> **GMAT Insider:** It is extremely unlikely that you will ever have to use the quadratic formula on the GMAT. It is much more useful to be comfortable factoring by inspection than it is to memorize the quadratic formula.

The equation can also be solved with the quadratic formula as follows:

$$y = -5 + \frac{\sqrt{5^2 - 4 \cdot 3 \cdot 2}}{2 \cdot 3} = \frac{-5 + \sqrt{25 - 24}}{6} = \frac{-5 + 1}{6} = -\frac{4}{6}$$

and

$$y = \frac{-5 - \sqrt{5^2 - 4 \cdot 3 \cdot 2}}{2 \cdot 3} = \frac{-5 - \sqrt{25 - 24}}{6} = \frac{-5 - 1}{6} = -\frac{6}{6} = -1$$

Factoring Drill

A. $x^2 + 13x + 36 = 0$ Solve for x.

B. $x^2 - 6x - 27 = 0$ Solve for x.

Let's finish with a great GMAT problem that tests your overall understanding of quadratic equations:

8.   If 4 is one solution of the equation $x^2 + 3x + k = 10$, where k is a constant, what is the other solution?

(A)   -7

(B)   -4

(C)   -3

(D)   1

(E)   6

Drill Answers

A. $(x + 9)(x + 4) = 0$, so $x = -4$ or -9

B. $(x + 3)(x - 9) = 0$, so $x = -3$ or 9

Common Algebraic Equations

Memorize these three common algebraic equations:

1. $(x + y)^2 = (x + y)(x + y) = x^2 + 2xy + y^2$
2. $(x - y)^2 = (x - y)(x - y) = x^2 - 2xy + y^2$
3. $(x + y)(x - y) = x^2 - y^2$ -- called the *difference of squares*

GMAT Insider: Recognizing these common algebraic equations is one of the most important algebra skills on the GMAT.

Students should be very comfortable with these templates and be able to recognize both sides of these common equations. Let's try a few together.

Here is a medium-difficulty GMAT problem in which you need to recognize the difference of squares:

9. $(\sqrt{2} + 1)(\sqrt{2} - 1)(\sqrt{3} + 1)(\sqrt{3} - 1) =$

(A)   2

(B)   3

(C) $2\sqrt{6}$

(D)   5

(E)   6

Habits of Great Test Takers: One sure route to confidence on the test is to practice the skills required for the test until they are second nature. Here, there is simply no substitute for study and practice, as all exams test "something" – some kind of knowledge that must be used to succeed. When test-takers are secure in that knowledge, they can more confidently and efficiently focus on the application of it, rather than the mere mental recollection of it. I suggest "minimizing what you memorize", and conceptually understanding the required skills whenever possible. For example, when I took the GMAT, I specifically remember blanking on an exponent property, then simply proving it to myself using smaller numbers. Because I understood exponents conceptually, I was able to confidently move on when my memory failed, rather than panicking that I had forgotten an important rule. Tests produce stress, and those who can confidently remember concepts and skills will be at a large advantage over those for whom nerves are more of an issue.
                    – Brian Galvin, LOS ANGELES

Inequalities

While the basic rules for inequalities are generally straightforward, Data Sufficiency questions with inequalities represent one of the hardest question types on the GMAT. In this section, you will be introduced to all of the important rules relating to inequalities, as well as some of the common tricks that the GMAT employs on inequality questions. In the Data Sufficiency lesson, we will reexamine this particular question type with numerous difficult examples.

Note
Because of the difficulty of inequality concepts on the GMAT and the time constraints of the class, this section has been designed for students to self-study. If there are concepts that you do not understand in the initial presentation, go back through this section at your own pace.

Rules and Definitions

What are inequalities? They are similar to normal algebraic equations, except the equal sign is substituted with one the following symbols:

A	$\neq$	B	A is not equal to B
A	$>$	B	A is greater than B
A	$\geq$	B	A is greater or equal to B
A	$<$	B	A is less than B
A	$\leq$	B	A is less or equal to B

Almost all rules that apply to equations also apply to inequalities (i.e. whatever operation you apply to one side of an equation, you have to apply to the other side). The most important difference with inequalities is that if you multiply or divide both sides by a negative number, the inequality sign must be flipped.

Your ability to properly apply rules is tested frequently on inequality questions. Let's break down the different operations that can be performed on inequalities to make sure you have a good understanding of these rules.

1. Addition and Subtraction

With addition and subtraction simply treat the inequality as an equation. Let's look at an example of an equation and an inequality:

$x + 3 = 2x + 5$ *To solve this equation, we combine like terms on each side to find that x = -2.*

$x + 3 > 2x + 5$ *To solve this inequality we follow the same steps and find that that x < -2.*

2. Multiplication or Division

With multiplication and division, treat the inequality as an equation if you are dividing or multiplying both sides by a positive number.

Let's look at a few examples to help understand the concept:

Take the simple inequality 5 > 3, which we know to be true. If you multiply both sides of this inequality by 5, you get the new inequality 25 > 15, which we know must also be true. Why? Because we followed the basic rules for equations and multiplied both sides by a positive number. As a result, we did not need to change the inequality sign.

However, consider the same example where we multiply both sides by -5. Now if we follow basic equation rules but don't change the sign, then the new inequality is -25 > -15. This inequality is not true. Why? On the number line, -25 is farther to the left than -15. Because -25 is more negative than -15, -25 is actually less than -15. When manipulating the original inequality we needed to flip the sign so that the correct end result would be -25 < -15, because the number we multiplied by was negative.

To understand what is going on when flipping the sign, it is helpful to look at a number line to see why when x > y then -x < -y.

Algebra

As with many other areas on the GMAT, these rules can be tested with very clever and very difficult questions. Let's look at a tricky data sufficiency problem that addresses the rules we just learned with multiplication and division.

10.   Is $x > 3y$?

   (1) $\frac{x}{y} > 3$

   (2) $y > 7$

(A)   Statement (1) ALONE is sufficient, but statement (2) alone is not sufficient.

(B)   Statement (2) ALONE is sufficient, but statement (1) alone is not sufficient.

(C)   BOTH statements TOGETHER are sufficient, but NEITHER statement ALONE is sufficient.

(D)   EACH statement ALONE is sufficient.

(E)   Statements (1) and (2) TOGETHER are NOT sufficient.

3. Combining inequalities

Just as with equations, you are allowed to add inequalities together, but only when the sign is pointing in the same direction.

Let's again look at an example with an equation and then an inequality:

We know that if we have the two equations below, we are allowed to simply sum the two equations, which cancels y and allows us to solve for x quickly:

$x + y = 12$
$x - y = 8$
$(x + y) + (x - y) = 12 + 8$
$2x = 20$ and $x = 10$

Facts & Formulas: You are not allowed to multiply or divide by a variable in an inequality problem unless you are sure whether the variable is positive or negative. Do not subtract inequalities! Subtracting an inequality would be the equivalent of multiplying it by -1, and would reverse the inequality sign. It is better simply better to always add inequalities.

With inequalities, we can also add them together but only when the sign within each inequality is pointing in the same direction:

$x + y > 12$

$x - y > 8$

$2x > 20$ and $x > 10$

Consider this harder example:

$x + y < 12$
$x - y > 8$

To combine these inequalities, we must first get the signs pointing in the same direction. To do this, manipulate the second inequality by multiplying by (-1) so that we can add them together and eliminate x.

$x - y > 8$

$(-1)(x - y) < (-1)(8)$ *(note flipping of sign)*

$-x + y < -8$

Now we can combine the manipulated inequality with the first.

$x + y < 12$
$(x + y) + (-x + y) < 12 + (-8)$
$2y < 4$ and $y < 2$

Note
There is no way to isolate *x* because there is no manipulation that will allow us to eliminate that variable and still have our inequality signs pointing in the same direction.

Algebra

4. Inequalities with absolute value

While there are two approaches to these types of inequality problems, the most reliable is to create two separate inequalities that consider the two possible scenarios given by the absolute value sign (positive/zero and negative). Consider the following two examples:

$|x| < 5$

In this case, the absolute value of x is less than 5 and there are two possible scenarios: either x is positive/zero or negative. If x is positive or zero, then the following case is true: x < 5. However, if x is negative, then the following inequality is true: –x < 5 or after manipulating by -1: x > -5. Taking them together we know that x < 5 and x > -5 which can also be written as -5 < x < 5. Here is the visual representation of that on the number line.

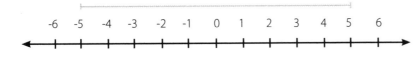

$|x| > 5$

In this case the absolute value of x is greater than 5 and again there are two possible scenarios. Either x is positive or negative. If x is positive, then the following case is true: x > 5. However, if x is negative then the following inequality is true: –x > 5 or after manipulating by -1; x < -5. Taking them together, we know that x > 5 or x < -5, which cannot be written as one statement. Here is the visual representation of that on the number line.

Summarized in simplistic terms, absolute values with inequalities can be considered in the following manner:

$|x| < y$ means $-y < x < y$ and $|x| > y$ means $x > y$ or $x < -y$

> *Facts & Formulas:* Recall from the Math Essentials lesson that the absolute value of a number refers to the distance on the number line from that number to zero. The absolute value of a positive number is itself. The absolute value of a negative number is the same number without the negative sign.
> $|3|=3$
> $|-3|=3$

Consider one last example where there is more than a variable within the absolute value sign:

$|x - 3| > 5$

Again we must consider the two scenarios. 1. When x - 3 is zero or greater and 2. When x - 3 is negative. In the first scenario, we know that x - 3 > 5 and x > 8. However, when the value of x - 3 is negative, we must consider the second scenario which is – (x - 3) > 5. After simplifying this inequality, we have –x + 3 > 5 or –x > 2 or x < -2. Putting these together, we know that x > 8 or x < -2.

While it is useful to understand conceptually what is going on, it is generally quicker to just use the template given on the previous page:

$|x| > y$ means $x > y$ or $x < -y$

From that you can see that $|x - 3| > 5$
$x - 3 > 5$ or $x - 3 < -5$

Simplifying, we see that $x > 8$ or $x < -2$.

Algebra

Functions

What is a function? It is simply another way to write an algebraic expression with one variable (the GMAT does not test multivariable functions). Take the expression $x^2 + 5$. The function f for that expression can be denoted by the following: $f(x) = x^2 + 5$. In simple language, think of the input in this function as the value of x and the output of this function as the value defined by the expression $x^2 + 5$ for that value of x. For this particular function, $f(2) = 9$ because $2^2 + 5 = 9$.

Functions can be expressed with any letter but on the GMAT it will generally be defined with $f(x)$ or $g(x)$. Let's look at a couple more examples of functions:

$$f(x) = \frac{x + 5}{\sqrt{x + 5}}$$ For this function, f(4) = 3 because $\frac{4 + 5}{\sqrt{4 + 5}} = \frac{9}{\sqrt{9}} = 3$

Note
The domain of a function is defined as the set of all allowable inputs for the function. In this function, the domain is restricted by the square root and by the denominator. In most function problems, the domain is the set of all real numbers. Here, the domain is all values of $x > -5$ because the square root of a negative number is not a real number, and because a value of 0 in the denominator would be undefined.

Here is one more example:

$$g(x) = (\sqrt[3]{x})(x + 5)$$

For this function, $g(8) = 26$, because $(\sqrt[3]{8})(8 + 5) = 2(13) = 26$

Note
In this problem the domain of the function is all real numbers, because the output of this function will be a real number for any real number value of x (the input).

Let's look at an example function problem from the GMAT:

11. The function *f* is defined by subtracting 25 from the square of a number and the function *g* is defined as the square root of one-half of a number. If *g(f(x))*= 10 then which of the following is a possible value of *x*?

(A)   -15

(B)   -5

(C)   0

(D)   5

(E)   25

Think Like the Test Maker: Function questions can be made more difficult by nesting one function within another. Just remember to begin with the outer function and treat each function as a separate step.

GMAT Insider: One trend on the GMAT seems to be more function questions, although it is unlikely that you will see more than one on any single test.

Note
Backsolving is a legitimate approach to this problem if you are unsure how to solve it in the textbook fashion. Simply apply the functions from the inside out to the 5 answer choices to see which one gives the desired result of 10.

The same question, but easier:

The function f is defined by subtracting 25 from the square of a number. If *f(x)* = 200 then which of the following is a possible value of *x*?

(A)   -15

(B)   -5

(C)   0

(D)   5

(E)   25

Assorted Problems

As in the Arithmetic Book, a number of problems in this book are categorized into different focus areas. Remember to check the solutions at the back of the book. Where appropriate shortcuts exist, we will also show the "lazy genius" approach. We begin with two specific kinds of function questions often seen on the GMAT.

Function Application Sequences

Sequences represent particular kinds of function problems on the GMAT. The domain of a sequence (its allowable input values) consists of the positive integers. The first term of a sequence is the output when the input is 1, the second term of a sequence is the output when the input is 2, etc.

The terms of the sequence are notated as $a_1, a_2, a_3, \ldots, a_n$. In the sequence $a_n = n^2$, the first term (a_1) is 1, the second term (a_2) is 4, and so on, such that the sequence is: 1, 4, 9, 16, 25, 36…

Consider the following question:

12.   The sequence $a_1, a_2, a_3, \ldots, a_n$ is defined by $a_n = a_{n-2} + a_{n-1}$ for all $n > 2$. If $a_3 = 2$ and $a_5 = 5$, what is the value of a_6?

(A)   7

(B)   8

(C)   10

(D)   12

(E)   13

Function Application Symbol Problems

The GMAT sometimes likes to give Quantitative problems that define and use unfamiliar symbols. This strategy is employed to confuse test takers, but you will be fine as long as you remember that despite the unfamiliar appearance, everything reduces to the same key concepts you already know. Simply plug in and carry out the operations as you normally would.

13.   If the operation € is defined for all x and y by the equation $x \mathbin{€} y = 2xy$, then $3 \mathbin{€} (4 \mathbin{€} 5) =$

(A)   80
(B)   120
(C)   160
(D)   240
(E)   360

Assorted Algebraic Word Problems and Equation Problems

GMAT Insider: Translating word problems into algebraic equations is one of the most important skills on the GMAT, and it is a major weakness for many students.

One of the most important skills on the GMAT is the ability to write proper algebraic equations from word problems. With these problems, we want students to build a solid foundation for creating equations from different word problems. We will look at many specialized and more difficult types of word problems in the Problem Solving Lesson.

14.   Miguel took a taxi to the airport and paid $2.50 to start plus $0.25 per mile. Sean took a different route and paid $2.50 plus $5.00 in bridge toll plus $0.25 per mile. If each was charged exactly the same amount, and Sean's ride was 30 miles, how long (in miles) was Miguel's ride?

(A)   10
(B)   20
(C)   30
(D)   40
(E)   50

Algebra

15. Elena purchased brand x pens for $4.00 apiece and brand y pens for $2.80 apiece. If Elena purchased a total of 12 of these pens for $42.00, how many brand x pens did she purchase?

(A)   4

(B)   5

(C)   6

(D)   7

(E)   8

16. If tank *x* contains only gasoline, how many kiloliters of gasoline are in tank *x*?

(1) If $\frac{1}{2}$ of the gasoline in tank *x* were pumped out, the tank would be filled to $\frac{1}{3}$ of its capacity.

(2) If 0.75 kiloliter of gasoline were pumped into tank *x*, it would be filled to capacity.

(A) Statement (1) ALONE is sufficient, but statement (2) alone is not sufficient.

(B) Statement (2) ALONE is sufficient, but statement (1) alone is not sufficient.

(C) BOTH statements TOGETHER are sufficient, but NEITHER statement ALONE is sufficient.

(D) EACH statement ALONE is sufficient.

(E) Statements (1) and (2) TOGETHER are NOT sufficient.

17. Missy ate *m* more crackers than Audrey did, from a box that originally contained *n* crackers. Together, they finished the box. Which of the following represents the number of crackers that Missy ate?

(A) $\dfrac{n+m}{2n}$

(B) $\dfrac{m-n}{2}$

(C) $\dfrac{n-m}{2}$

(D) $\dfrac{m+n}{2}$

(E) $\dfrac{n}{2+m}$

18.   If Jenna will be 48 years old 14 years from now, how old was she *x* years ago?

(A)   *x* - 34

(B)   *x* - 14

(C)   34 – *x*

(D)   62 - *x*

(E)   48 + *x*

19.   How many hours does it take Jennifer to run y miles if she runs at a speed of x miles an hour?

(A) $\dfrac{x}{y}$

(B) $\dfrac{y}{x}$

(C) xy

(D) $\dfrac{60x}{y}$

(E) $\dfrac{y}{60x}$

20. How many more men than women are in the room?

   (1) There is a total of 20 women and men in the room.

   (2) The number of men in the room equals the square of the number of women in the room.

(A) Statement (1) ALONE is sufficient, but statement (2) alone is not sufficient.

(B) Statement (2) ALONE is sufficient, but statement (1) alone is not sufficient.

(C) BOTH statements TOGETHER are sufficient, but NEITHER statement ALONE is sufficient.

(D) EACH statement ALONE is sufficient.

(E) Statements (1) and (2) TOGETHER are NOT sufficient.

21.   What is the number of female employees in Company *x*?

(1)   If Company *x* were to hire 14 more people and all of these people were females, the ratio of the number of male employees to the number of female employees would then be 16 to 9.

(2)   Company *x* has 105 more male employees than female employees.

(A)   Statement (1) ALONE is sufficient, but statement (2) alone is not sufficient.

(B)   Statement (2) ALONE is sufficient, but statement (1) alone is not sufficient.

(C)   BOTH statements TOGETHER are sufficient, but NEITHER statement ALONE is sufficient.

(D)   EACH statement ALONE is sufficient.

(E)   Statements (1) and (2) TOGETHER are NOT sufficient.

22. Each person on a committee with 40 members voted for exactly one of 3 candidates, F, G, or H. Did Candidate F receive the most votes from the 40 votes cast?

(1) Candidate F received 11 of the votes.

(2) Candidate H received 14 of the votes.

(A) Statement (1) ALONE is sufficient, but statement (2) alone is not sufficient.

(B) Statement (2) ALONE is sufficient, but statement (1) alone is not sufficient.

(C) BOTH statements TOGETHER are sufficient, but NEITHER statement ALONE is sufficient.

(D) EACH statement ALONE is sufficient.

(E) Statements (1) and (2) TOGETHER are NOT sufficient.

Algebra

23.   There are 1,600 jelly beans divided between two jars (*x* and *y*). If there are 100 fewer jelly beans in jar *x* than three times the number of beans in jar *y*, how many beans are in jar *x*?

(A)   375

(B)   950

(C)   1,150

(D)   1,175

(E)   1,350

24. If John takes 12 minutes to eat x hotdogs, how many seconds will it take him to eat z hotdogs, assuming he continues to eat at the same rate?

(A) $\frac{720z}{x}$

(B) $\frac{12x}{z}$

(C) $\frac{x}{12z}$

(D) $\frac{720}{xz}$

(E) $\frac{xz}{12}$

25. On the number line, if $w > x$, y is the midpoint between w and z, and x is twice as far from z as it is from w, then $\frac{w - y}{z - x}$ could equal which of the following?

(A)   -2

(B) $-\frac{1}{4}$

(C)   0

(D) $\frac{1}{4}$

(E) $1\frac{1}{2}$

26.   Marcia's bucket can hold a maximum of how many liters of water?

(1)   The bucket currently contains 9 liters of water.

(2)   If 3 liters of water are added to the bucket when it is half full of water, the amount of water in the bucket will increase by $\frac{1}{3}$.

(A)   Statement (1) ALONE is sufficient, but statement (2) alone is not sufficient.

(B)   Statement (2) ALONE is sufficient, but statement (1) alone is not sufficient.

(C)   BOTH statements TOGETHER are sufficient, but NEITHER statement ALONE is sufficient.

(D)   EACH statement ALONE is sufficient.

(E)   Statements (1) and (2) TOGETHER are NOT sufficient.

27.   A number x is multiplied by 3, and this product is then divided by 5. If the positive square root of the result of these two operations equals x, what is the value of x if $x \neq 0$?

(A) $\dfrac{25}{9}$

(B) $\dfrac{9}{5}$

(C) $\dfrac{5}{3}$

(D) $\dfrac{3}{5}$

(E) $\dfrac{9}{25}$

28. The sum of the heights of two high-rises is x feet. If the first high rise is 37 feet taller than the second, how tall will the second high rise be after they add an antenna with a height of z feet to the top?

(A) $\dfrac{(x + z)}{2 + 37}$

(B) $2x - (37 + z)$

(C) $\dfrac{(x - 37)}{2} + z$

(D) $\dfrac{x}{2} - 37 + z$

(E) $\dfrac{(2x - 37)}{z}$

29. Two accountants, Rhodes and Smith, went to a business meeting together. Rhodes drove to the meeting and Smith drove back from the meeting. If Rhodes and Smith each drove 140 kilometers, what was the average speed, in kilometers per hour, at which Rhodes drove?

    (1)   The average speed at which Smith drove was 70 kilometers per hour.

    (2)   Rhodes drove for exactly 2 hours.

(A)   Statement (1) ALONE is sufficient, but statement (2) alone is not sufficient.

(B)   Statement (2) ALONE is sufficient, but statement (1) alone is not sufficient.

(C)   BOTH statements TOGETHER are sufficient, but NEITHER statement ALONE is sufficient.

(D)   EACH statement ALONE is sufficient.

(E)   Statements (1) and (2) TOGETHER are NOT sufficient.

30. What percent of the employees of Company *x* are technicians?

   (1)   Exactly 40 percent of the men and 55 percent of the women employed by Company *x* are technicians.

   (2)   At Company *x*, the ratio of the number of technicians to the number of non-technicians is 9 to 11.

(A)   Statement (1) ALONE is sufficient, but statement (2) alone is not sufficient.

(B)   Statement (2) ALONE is sufficient, but statement (1) alone is not sufficient.

(C)   BOTH statements TOGETHER are sufficient, but NEITHER statement ALONE is sufficient.

(D)   EACH statement ALONE is sufficient.

(E)   Statements (1) and (2) TOGETHER are NOT sufficient.

31.   On a certain day it took Bill three times as long to drive from home to work as it took Sue to drive from home to work. How many kilometers did Bill drive from home to work?

(1)   Sue drove 10 kilometers from home to work, and the ratio of $\dfrac{\text{distance driven from home to work}}{\text{time to drive from home to work}}$ was the same for Bill and Sue that day.

(2)   The ratio of $\dfrac{\text{distance driven from home to work}}{\text{time to drive from home to work}}$ for Sue that day was 64 kilometers per hour.

(A)   Statement (1) ALONE is sufficient, but statement (2) alone is not sufficient.

(B)   Statement (2) ALONE is sufficient, but statement (1) alone is not sufficient.

(C)   BOTH statements TOGETHER are sufficient, but NEITHER statement ALONE is sufficient.

(D)   EACH statement ALONE is sufficient.

(E)   Statements (1) and (2) TOGETHER are NOT sufficient.

32.   If $x = 5 - 4k$ and $y = 5k - 3$, then for what value of k does $x = y$?

(A)   0

(B) $\dfrac{8}{9}$

(C) $\dfrac{9}{8}$

(D)   2

(E)   8

Exponents and Roots

33.   If $(5^k)^{\frac{7}{3}} = 25$, what is the value of k?

(A) $\frac{3}{7}$

(B) $\frac{5}{7}$

(C) $\frac{3}{5}$

(D) $\frac{6}{7}$

(E) $\frac{7}{5}$

34. If $x^3 = 115$, the value of x must be which of the following?

(A) less than 4

(B) between 4 and 5

(C) between 6 and 7

(D) between 8 and 9

(E) between 9 and 10

35.   If $(2^x)(2^y) = 8$ and $(9^x)(3^y) = 81$, then (x, y) equals which of the following?

(A)   (1,2)

(B)   (2,1)

(C)   (1,1)

(D)   (2,2)

(E)   (1,3)

36. If $\dfrac{(0.0024 \cdot 10^{j})}{(0.08 \cdot 10^{r})} = 3 \cdot 10^{6}$ then $j - r$ equals which of the following?

(A)   9

(B)   8

(C)   7

(D)   6

(E)   5

37.   If $3^x - 3^{(x-1)} = (3)^{13} (2)$, what is the value of x?

(A)   8

(B)   10

(C)   13

(D)   14

(E)   15

38.   For how many integers n is $n + n = n \cdot n$?

(A)   None

(B)   One

(C)   Two

(D)   Three

(E)   More than three

39.   If *n* is an integer and 1< *n* <100, what is the value of *n*?

    (1)   *n* is the square of an integer.

    (2)   *n* is the fourth power of an integer.

(A)   Statement (1) ALONE is sufficient, but statement (2) alone is not sufficient.

(B)   Statement (2) ALONE is sufficient, but statement (1) alone is not sufficient.

(C)   BOTH statements TOGETHER are sufficient, but NEITHER statement ALONE is sufficient.

(D)   EACH statement ALONE is sufficient.

(E)   Statements (1) and (2) TOGETHER are NOT sufficient.

40. $$\frac{x^{-5}(x^4)^2 x^3}{x(x^{-7})(x^{-5})^4}$$

The above equation may be re-written as which of the following?

(A) $\dfrac{1}{x^{25}}$

(B) $\dfrac{1}{x^8}$

(C) x^6

(D) x^{20}

(E) x^{32}

41.   If $x = 5^{25}$ and $x^x = 5^k$, what is k?

(A) 5^{26}

(B) 5^{27}

(C) 5^{50}

(D) 5^{52}

(E) 5^{625}

42. What is the value of $\left(\sqrt[3]{\sqrt{\sqrt[3]{\sqrt{512}}}}\right)^2$?

(A) $\dfrac{1}{16}$

(B) $\dfrac{1}{8}$

(C) $\dfrac{1}{2}$

(D) 2

(E) 8

43.   If x and y are positive integers and $x^y = x^{2y-3}$, what is the value of x^y ?

(1) $x = 2$

(2) $x^3 = 8$

(A)   Statement (1) ALONE is sufficient, but statement (2) alone is not sufficient.

(B)   Statement (2) ALONE is sufficient, but statement (1) alone is not sufficient.

(C)   BOTH statements TOGETHER are sufficient, but NEITHER statement ALONE is sufficient.

(D)   EACH statement ALONE is sufficient.

(E)   Statements (1) and (2) TOGETHER are NOT sufficient.

44.   If $5 \cdot \sqrt[x]{125} = \dfrac{1}{5^{\frac{1}{x}}}$, then $x =$

(A)   -4

(B) $\dfrac{-1}{\sqrt{2}}$

(C)   0

(D) $\dfrac{1}{\sqrt{2}}$

(E)   1

45. $\dfrac{(.08)^{-4}}{(.04)^{-3}} =$

(A) $\dfrac{-16}{25}$

(B) $\dfrac{16}{25}$

(C) $\dfrac{25}{16}$

(D) 16

(E) 25

46. If m is an integer such that $(-2)^{2m} = 2^{9-m}$, then $m =$

(A)   1

(B)   2

(C)   3

(D)   4

(E)   6

Algebraic Calculations

In the online Math Essentials lesson, there were many drills to test your ability with algebraic calculations. If you are already comfortable with most algebraic calculations, use the easier questions in this section to work on speed.

47.   If $\dfrac{x}{x+y} = 6$, then $\dfrac{y}{y+x} =$

(A)   -5

(B) $\dfrac{5}{11}$

(C)   1

(D) $\dfrac{11}{5}$

(E)   5

48.   If $\dfrac{3.5}{0.25 + x} = 10$, then $x =$

(A)   -3.7

(B)   0.1

(C)   0.3

(D)   0.5

(E)   2.8

49. $\dfrac{2(x-2)}{5} + \dfrac{24-12x}{6} + 2x = \dfrac{4x}{5} + 3$. Solve for x.

(A) 0

(B) 0.5

(C) 1

(D) 1.5

(E) 2

50.   If $\dfrac{4-x}{2+x} = x$, what is the value of $x^2 + 3x - 4$?

(A)   -4

(B)   -1

(C)   0

(D)   1

(E)   2

51. $(\sqrt{11} + \sqrt{11} + \sqrt{11})^2 =$

(A)   363

(B)   121

(C)   99

(D)   66

(E)   33

52. $x - 10z = 3y + 67$
     $2y - x + 5z = -17$
     $5z - y = 2x + 100$

Solve for z.

(A) $-\dfrac{29}{5}$

(B) $-\dfrac{13}{5}$

(C) $-\dfrac{8}{5}$

(D) $\dfrac{13}{5}$

(E) $\dfrac{29}{5}$

53.   If $k \neq 0$ and $\dfrac{z^2}{k} + 4z + 3 = \dfrac{z}{k}$, then $k =$

(A) $\dfrac{z^2 - 3}{4}$

(B) $\dfrac{-z^2 + 4z}{3}$

(C) $-z(z + 4)3$

(D) $\dfrac{z - z^2}{4z + 3}$

(E) $z^2 + 4z - 3$

54. $y = 17x + 32$
$x = 3 - y + 2x$

Solve for y.

(A) $-\dfrac{29}{16}$

(B) $-\dfrac{19}{16}$

(C) 0

(D) $\dfrac{19}{16}$

(E) $\dfrac{29}{16}$

55.   If $(b - 3)\left(4 + \dfrac{2}{b}\right) = 0$ and $b \neq 3$, then $b =$

(A)   -8

(B)   -2

(C) $-\dfrac{1}{2}$

(D) $\dfrac{1}{2}$

(E)   2

56. Which of the following equations is NOT equivalent to $25x^2 = y^2 - 4$?

(A) $25x^2 + 4 = y^2$

(B) $75x^2 = 3y^2 - 12$

(C) $25x^2 = (y + 2)(y - 2)$

(D) $5x = y - 2$

(E) $x^2 = \dfrac{(y^2 - 4)}{25}$

57.   If x, y, and z are positive, is $x = \dfrac{y}{z^2}$?

(1) $z = \dfrac{y}{xz}$

(2) $z = \sqrt{\dfrac{y}{x}}$

(A)   Statement (1) ALONE is sufficient, but statement (2) alone is not sufficient.

(B)   Statement (2) ALONE is sufficient, but statement (1) alone is not sufficient.

(C)   BOTH statements TOGETHER are sufficient, but NEITHER statement ALONE is sufficient.

(D)   EACH statement ALONE is sufficient.

(E)   Statements (1) and (2) TOGETHER are NOT sufficient.

58.   If $x = -1$, then $-(x^4 + x^3 + x^2 + x) =$

(A)   -10

(B)   -4

(C)   0

(D)   4

(E)   10

59.   If $x > 5{,}999$, then the value of $\dfrac{2x}{5x+1}$ is closest to which of the following?

(A) $\dfrac{2}{7}$

(B) $\dfrac{2}{5}$

(C) $\dfrac{12}{31}$

(D) $\dfrac{12}{6}$

(E) $\dfrac{12}{5}$

60.   Of the following, which is least?

(A) $\dfrac{1}{0.2}$

(B) $(0.2)^2$

(C)   0.02

(D) $\dfrac{0.2}{2}$

(E)   0.2

$$S = \dfrac{\dfrac{2}{n}}{\dfrac{1}{x} + \dfrac{2}{3x}}$$

61.   In the expression above, if $xn \neq 0$, what is the value of S ?

(1) $x = 2n$

(2) $n = \dfrac{1}{2}$

(A)   Statement (1) ALONE is sufficient, but statement (2) alone is not sufficient.

(B)   Statement (2) ALONE is sufficient, but statement (1) alone is not sufficient.

(C)   BOTH statements TOGETHER are sufficient, but NEITHER statement ALONE is sufficient.

(D)   EACH statement ALONE is sufficient.

(E)   Statements (1) and (2) TOGETHER are NOT sufficient.

Algebraic Number Properties

62.   Is 2^x greater than 100 ?

    (1) $2^{\sqrt{x}} = 8$

    (2) $\frac{1}{2^x} < 0.01$

(A)   Statement (1) ALONE is sufficient, but statement (2) alone is not sufficient.

(B)   Statement (2) ALONE is sufficient, but statement (1) alone is not sufficient.

(C)   BOTH statements TOGETHER are sufficient, but NEITHER statement ALONE is sufficient.

(D)   EACH statement ALONE is sufficient.

(E)   Statements (1) and (2) TOGETHER are NOT sufficient.

63.   If $x^3 = xy$ and $x \neq 0$, which of the following must be true?

I. $x = 2$
II. $x^2 = y$
III. $y = 1$

(A)   I only

(B)   II only

(C)   III only

(D)   I and III only

(E)   II and III

64.   What is the units digit of 2^{39}?

(A)   2

(B)   4

(C)   6

(D)   8

(E)   9

65.   If *m* is the product of all integers from 1 to 40, inclusive, what is the greatest
       integer *p* for which 10^p is a factor of *m*?

(A)   7

(B)   8

(C)   9

(D)   10

(E)   11

66.   What is the units digit of $9^{19} - 7^{15}$?

(A)   2

(B)   4

(C)   5

(D)   6

(E)   7

67.   What is the sum of all digits for the number $10^{30} - 37$?

(A)   63

(B)   252

(C)   261

(D)   270

(E)   337

68.   What is the value of the positive integer n ?

(1) $n^4 < 25$

(2) $n \neq n^2$

(A)   Statement (1) ALONE is sufficient, but statement (2) alone is not sufficient.

(B)   Statement (2) ALONE is sufficient, but statement (1) alone is not sufficient.

(C)   BOTH statements TOGETHER are sufficient, but NEITHER statement ALONE is sufficient.

(D)   EACH statement ALONE is sufficient.

(E)   Statements (1) and (2) TOGETHER are NOT sufficient.

69.   Is $x > y$?

   (1) $x^2 > y^2$

   (2) $x - y > 0$

(A)   Statement (1) ALONE is sufficient, but statement (2) alone is not sufficient.

(B)   Statement (2) ALONE is sufficient, but statement (1) alone is not sufficient.

(C)   BOTH statements TOGETHER are sufficient, but NEITHER statement ALONE is sufficient.

(D)   EACH statement ALONE is sufficient.

(E)   Statements (1) and (2) TOGETHER are NOT sufficient.

70. What is the units digit of $(23)^6(17)^3(61)^9$?

(A) 1

(B) 3

(C) 5

(D) 7

(E) 9

71.   If $x^2 + y^2 = 100, x \geq 0$, and $y \geq 0$, the maximum value of $x + y$ must be which of the following?

(A)   Less than 10

(B)   Greater or equal to 10 and less than 14

(C)   Greater than 14 and less than 19

(D)   Greater than 19 and Less than 23

(E)   Greater than 23

72. If $y = -\dfrac{x^3}{27}$, for what value of x is y the greatest?

(A)   -27

(B)   -3

(C)   0

(D)   3

(E)   27

73.   If *x* and *y* are positive integers, is the product *xy* divisible by 9?

    (1)   The product *xy* is divisible by 6.

    (2)   *x* and *y* are perfect squares.

(A)   Statement (1) ALONE is sufficient, but statement (2) alone is not sufficient.

(B)   Statement (2) ALONE is sufficient, but statement (1) alone is not sufficient.

(C)   BOTH statements TOGETHER are sufficient, but NEITHER statement ALONE is sufficient.

(D)   EACH statement ALONE is sufficient.

(E)   Statements (1) and (2) TOGETHER are NOT sufficient.

74.   If $3^x4^y = 177,147$ and $x - y = 11$, then $x =$

(A)   undefined

(B)   0

(C)   11

(D)   177,136

(E)   177,158

75.   What is $\sqrt{x^2 y^2}$ if $x < 0$ and $y > 0$?

(A) $-xy$

(B) xy

(C) $-|xy|$

(D) $|y|x$

(E)   no solution

76. If $y \neq 0$ and $y \neq -1$, which is greater, $\dfrac{x}{y}$ or $\dfrac{x}{y+1}$?

   (1) $x \neq 0$

   (2) $x > y$

(A)   Statement (1) ALONE is sufficient, but statement (2) alone is not sufficient.

(B)   Statement (2) ALONE is sufficient, but statement (1) alone is not sufficient.

(C)   BOTH statements TOGETHER are sufficient, but NEITHER statement ALONE is sufficient.

(D)   EACH statement ALONE is sufficient.

(E)   Statements (1) and (2) TOGETHER are NOT sufficient.

Algebra

77.   If n is a positive integer, then $n(n + 1)(n + 2)$ is which of the following?

(A)   even only when n is even

(B)   even only when n is odd

(C)   odd whenever n is odd

(D)   divisible by 3 only when n is odd

(E)   divisible by 12 whenever n is even

Common Algebraic Equations
(Quadratics, Difference of Squares, etc.)

78.   Which of the following equations has a root in common with $x^2 - 7x + 12 = 0$?

(A) $x^2 + 1 = 0$

(B) $x^2 - x - 12 = 0$

(C) $x^2 - 8x - 4 = 0$

(D) $3x^2 - 9 = 0$

(E) $x^2 + x - 6 = 0$

79.   If the expression $x^2 - \dfrac{xy}{5} + 25$ can be expressed by $(x - 5)^2$, what is the value of y?

(A)   0

(B)   5

(C)   25

(D)   50

(E) $\dfrac{5}{x}$

80. $3x^2 - 5x + 3 = 0$
Solve for x.

(A) $x = \dfrac{4}{3}$ or $x = \dfrac{1}{3}$

(B) $x = 2$ or $x = -\dfrac{1}{3}$

(C) $x = \dfrac{5}{6}$ or $x = \dfrac{1}{6}$

(D) $x = 0$ or $x = -3$

(E) No solution.

81.   Is $x^2 - y^2$ a positive number?

    (1) $x - y$ is a positive number.

    (2) $x + y$ is a positive number.

(A)   Statement (1) ALONE is sufficient, but statement (2) alone is not sufficient.

(B)   Statement (2) ALONE is sufficient, but statement (1) alone is not sufficient.

(C)   BOTH statements TOGETHER are sufficient, but NEITHER statement ALONE is sufficient.

(D)   EACH statement ALONE is sufficient.

(E)   Statements (1) and (2) TOGETHER are NOT sufficient.

82.   If x is positive, then $\dfrac{1}{\sqrt{x+1}+\sqrt{x}} =$

(A)   1

(B) x

(C) $\dfrac{1}{x}$

(D) $\sqrt{x+1} - \sqrt{x}$

(E) $\sqrt{x+1} + \sqrt{x}$

83. $999,999^2 - 1 =$

(A) $10^{10} - 2$

(B) $(10^6 - 2)^2$

(C) $10^5(10^6 - 2)$

(D) $10^6(10^5 - 2)$

(E) $10^6(10^6 - 2)$

Inequalities

84. If $b < 2$ and $2x - 3b = 0$, which of the following must be true?

(A) $x > -3$

(B) $x < 2$

(C) $x = 3$

(D) $x < 3$

(E) $x > 3$

85.   A fisherman, 15 miles from port, decides to try fishing somewhere else. He
        motors 3 miles in one direction in search of a school of fish, and then follows
        that school of fish for another 6 miles. If he is then x miles from port, what is
        the range of possible values for x?

(A) $3 \leq x \leq 9$

(B) $3 \leq x \leq 18$

(C) $6 \leq x \leq 24$

(D) $9 \leq x \leq 24$

(E) $12 \leq x \leq 25$

86.   If $-1 < x < 1$ and $x \neq 0$, which of the following inequalities must be true?

I. $x^3 < x$
II. $x^2 < |x|$
III. $x^4 - x^5 > x^3 - x^2$

(A)   I only

(B)   II only

(C)   III only

(D)   II and III only

(E)   I, II, and III

87.   If *x* is an integer, what is the value of *x*?

(1) $-2(x + 5) < -1$

(2) $-3x > 9$

(A)   Statement (1) ALONE is sufficient, but statement (2) alone is not sufficient.

(B)   Statement (2) ALONE is sufficient, but statement (1) alone is not sufficient.

(C)   BOTH statements TOGETHER are sufficient, but NEITHER statement ALONE is sufficient.

(D)   EACH statement ALONE is sufficient.

(E)   Statements (1) and (2) TOGETHER are NOT sufficient.

88.   Which of the following inequalities is equivalent to $x > -4$?

(A) $-5x + 3 < 15 - 2x$

(B) $1.75x - 4 < 0.25x - 10$

(C) $-2x + 2 < 2(x - 2) - 2x - 2$

(D) $4(x - 4) < 10(4 - x)$

(E)   None of the above.

89.   If -2 ≤ *m* ≤ 0 and *n* > 19, which of the following CANNOT be the value of *mn* ?

(A)   -48

(B)   -38

(C)   -20

(D)   0

(E)   19

90. If x is an integer, what is the value of x?

(1) $\dfrac{1}{5} < \dfrac{1}{1+x} < \dfrac{1}{2}$

(2) $(x - 3)(x - 4) = 0$

(A) Statement (1) ALONE is sufficient, but statement (2) alone is not sufficient.

(B) Statement (2) ALONE is sufficient, but statement (1) alone is not sufficient.

(C) BOTH statements TOGETHER are sufficient, but NEITHER statement ALONE is sufficient.

(D) EACH statement ALONE is sufficient.

(E) Statements (1) and (2) TOGETHER are NOT sufficient.

91.   If *x* and *y* are integers and $y = |x + 3| + |4 - x|$, does *y* equal 7 ?

        (1) $x < 4$

        (2) $x > -3$

(A)   Statement (1) ALONE is sufficient, but statement (2) alone is not sufficient.

(B)   Statement (2) ALONE is sufficient, but statement (1) alone is not sufficient.

(C)   BOTH statements TOGETHER are sufficient, but NEITHER statement ALONE is sufficient.

(D)   EACH statement ALONE is sufficient.

(E)   Statements (1) and (2) TOGETHER are NOT sufficient.

92. Is y a positive number?

(1) $2x + y > 27$

(2) $x - 3y < 24$

(A) Statement (1) ALONE is sufficient, but statement (2) alone is not sufficient.

(B) Statement (2) ALONE is sufficient, but statement (1) alone is not sufficient.

(C) BOTH statements TOGETHER are sufficient, but NEITHER statement ALONE is sufficient.

(D) EACH statement ALONE is sufficient.

(E) Statements (1) and (2) TOGETHER are NOT sufficient.

93.   Is $xy > 0$?

   (1) $x - y > -5$

   (2) $x - 2y < -7$

(A)   Statement (1) ALONE is sufficient, but statement (2) alone is not sufficient.

(B)   Statement (2) ALONE is sufficient, but statement (1) alone is not sufficient.

(C)   BOTH statements TOGETHER are sufficient, but NEITHER statement ALONE
        is sufficient.

(D)   EACH statement ALONE is sufficient.

(E)   Statements (1) and (2) TOGETHER are NOT sufficient.

Function Questions

94.   For all numbers q and r, the operation ¤ is defined by $q ¤ r = (q + 3)(r - 2)$.
        If $1 ¤ z = -8$, z is equal to which of the following?

(A)   -3

(B)   -2

(C)   -1

(D)   0

(E)   2

95.   If g is a function defined for all x by $g(x) = \frac{x^4}{16}$ then what is the value of $g(2x)$ in terms of $g(x)$?

(A) $\frac{g(x)}{16}$

(B) $\frac{g(x)}{4}$

(C) $4g(x)$

(D) $8g(x)$

(E) $16g(x)$

96. For which of the following functions is $g(c - d) = g(c) - g(d)$ for all positive numbers c and d?

(A)　　$g(x) = x^3$

(B)　　$g(x) = x + 5$

(C)　　$g(x) = \sqrt{3x}$

(D)　　$g(x) = 5x$

(E)　　$g(x) = \dfrac{15}{x}$

Solutions

Lesson

1. **(B)**

Step One: Do the prime factorization of 27 to get $3^{3(2x+4)} = 3^{3x+9}$

Step Two: Remove Parentheses $3^{6x+12} = 3^{3x+9}$

Step Three: Equate exponents $6x + 12 = 3x + 9$ and solve for $x = -1$

2. **(E)**

Step One: Factor numbers into their primes $(5^2 \cdot 3)^y(3^3)^{2y+1} = 5^4 3^x$

Step Two: Apply parentheses/distribution exponent rules to simplify: $5^{2y} \cdot 3^y \cdot 3^{6y+3} = 5^4 3^x$

Step Three: Combine like bases so each side of the equation is identical: $5^{2y} \cdot 3^{7y+3} = 5^4 3^x$

Step Four: Equate exponents as we learned from the exponent/factoring section: $2y = 4$ and $7y + 3 = x$. $y = 2$, so $x = 17$.

3. **(E)**

When adding or subtracting numbers or variables, you can only combine like terms. For instance, you cannot combine $x + y + 4$ as there are no like terms. However, take the example $2x + 3x + 4x$; it is possible to combine the like terms together to get $9x$. In this problem, think of 2^{4x} as the variable y. $y + y + y + y = 4y$. So, $2^{4x} + 2^{4x} + 2^{4x} + 2^{4x} = 4(2^{4x})$. Now, the equation looks like this: $4(2^{4x}) = 4^{24}$. You can now use your exponent rules to solve. Manipulate the equation to get like bases on each side: $2^2 \cdot 2^{4x} = (2^2)^{24}$ and combine to get $2^{4x+2} = 2^{48}$. As both sides now have identical bases, you can equate the exponents and solve for x. $4x + 2 = 48$, so $x = \frac{46}{4} = 11\frac{2}{4} = 11.5$. Alternately, you can also factor out a 2^{4x} from the left side of the equation which give you $2^{4x}(1 + 1 + 1 + 1) = 4^{24}$. Then combine the numbers in the parentheses to get $4(2^{4x}) = 4^{24}$. Then solve for x as explained previously.

4. (D)

Step One: Pull out all the perfect squares $= \sqrt{49 \cdot 2} + \sqrt{16 \cdot 2} + \sqrt{4 \cdot 2} = 7\sqrt{2} + 4\sqrt{2} + 2\sqrt{2}$

Step Two: Use your understanding of factoring to combine like terms: $13\sqrt{2}$

5. (C)

Statement (1) implies that x and y do not equal 0, since the product is not equal to zero. x^2 must be greater than zero because the square of any nonzero number is positive. A positive number times a negative number equals a negative number; thus $y^3 < 0$ since $x^2 y^3 < 0$. Likewise, if $y^3 < 0$, $y < 0$. However, (1) is not sufficient to determine whether $xy < 0$ because you do not know whether $x > 0$ or $x < 0$; thus, the answer is (B), (C), or (E). Similarly, from (2) alone you know that $x > 0$ since $xy^2 > 0$ and $y^2 > 0$, but you do not know whether $y > 0$ or $y < 0$. Combining the information from (1) and (2), you know $y < 0$ and $x > 0$. Thus, $xy < 0$ and the answer is (C).

6. (C)

If x is positive, then dividing both sides of $x^2 < x$ by x yields $x < 1$. If x is 0, $x^2 = x$, so the condition is not satisfied. If x is negative, then x^2 is positive, and $x^2 > x$, so the condition is not satisfied. Thus, we need to find an x such that $0 < x < 1$. C is the only answer choice in that range, so the answer is (C).

7. (A)

Starting with $\frac{5 + 5\sqrt{5}}{10 + \sqrt{500}}$, we notice that $500 = 100 \cdot 5$. Thus, $\sqrt{500} = \sqrt{100 \cdot 5} = 10\sqrt{5}$. So, the full equation reads: $\frac{5 + 5\sqrt{5}}{10 + 10\sqrt{5}} = \frac{5 + 5\sqrt{5}}{2(5 + 5\sqrt{5})}$. Dividing both top and bottom of the fraction by $5 + 5\sqrt{5}$, we get the answer of $\frac{1}{2}$.

Algebra

8. **(A)**

In this problem, one must use the given information by inserting it into the equation and solving for k, the constant. If 4 is one solution of the equation, then $4^2 + 3(4) + k = 10$ and $k = -18$. Thus, the equation to be solved is $x^2 + 3x - 18 = 10$ or $x^2 + 3x - 28 = 0$. Factoring the quadratic yields $(x + 7)(x – 4)= 0$, which has solutions -7 and 4. Therefore, $x = -7$ is the other solution, and the answer is (A). **Shortcut:** A second, faster way to solve this one is to do so without first solving for k. $x^2 + 3x +(k - 10)= 0$. The two factors must multiply to $(k - 10)$ and must add to $+ 3$. Since one of the factors was already given as $(x - 4)$, the only possiblity to yield the sum of $+ 3$ is $(x + 7)$.

9. **(A)**

From the relationship $(a + b)(a – b) = a^2 – b^2$, the following can be derived:
$(\sqrt{2} + 1)(\sqrt{2} - 1) = 2 - 1 = 1$ and $(\sqrt{3} + 1)(\sqrt{3} - 1) = 3 - 1 = 2$
Thus, $(\sqrt{2} + 1)(\sqrt{2} - 1)(\sqrt{3} + 1)(\sqrt{3} - 1) = (1)(2) = 2$. The correct answer choice is (A).

10. **(C)**

Many students want to pick (A) in this problem because they think that if $\frac{x}{y} > 3$, then they can simply multiply both sides of the inequality by y to get $x > 3y$, which precisely answers the question. However, because we do not know the sign of y we cannot multiply both sides by the variable as we do not know whether we should flip the sign or not. In other words, the first statement is sufficient, if and only if, we know that y is positive or negative. The second statement is clearly insufficient by itself, but it does let us know that y is positive. Taking them together we are allowed to make the needed manipulation to show that $x > 3y$ and the answer is (C).

11. **(A)**

With multiple function questions simply separate the problem into two parts. First consider the outer function g. If you are working with $g(f(x))$, $f(x)$ becomes the input for the function g. Therefore $g(f(x)) = \sqrt{\frac{f(x)}{2}}$, and since $g(f(x)) = 10$, $\sqrt{\frac{f(x)}{2}} = 10$. We can now solve for

$f(x)$ by squaring both sides and we see that $f(x) = 200$. In the problem $f(x)$ is defined as

$x^2 - 25$. Therefore $x^2 - 25 = 200$ and $x^2 = 225$. Here there are two possible inputs or values

for x: 15 or -15.

Assorted Problems

12. (B)

This particular sequence may look familiar to some students: it is known as the Fibonacci

sequence. Begin with a_5. According to the definition of the sequence, $a_5 = a_3 + a_4$, or

$5 = 2 + a_4$. Therefore $a_4 = 3$. Then, again according to the definition, $a_6 = 3 + 5 = 8$.

13. (D)

Begin with the operation inside the parentheses. $4 \in 5 = 2(4)(5) = 40$.

Then $3 \in 40 = 2(3)(40) = 240$.

14. (E)

M is what Miguel paid, m is the distance Miguel traveled (in miles). S is what Sean paid,

and s is the distance he traveled (in miles). Converting the text in the problem to algebra

yields: $M = 2.50 + 0.25 \cdot m$ (for Miguel's trip)

$S = 2.50 + 5.00 + 0.25 \cdot s = 7.50 + 0.25 \cdot s$ (for Sean's trip)

$M = S; s = 30$

Setting $M = S$, gives: $2.50 + \frac{m}{4} = 7.50 + \frac{s}{4}$

Solve for m: $\frac{m}{4} = 7.50 - 2.50 + \frac{s}{4}$

$\frac{m}{4} = 5.00 + \frac{s}{4}$

$m = 20 + s$

Plug in 30 for s to get $m = 50$. The correct answer is (E).

15. **(D)**

Let x denote the number of brand x pens Elena purchased. Then the number of brand y pens she purchased was $12 - x$ and the total cost of the pens was $4x + 2.80(12 - x) = 42.00$ dollars. This equation can be solved as follows in the progression below:

$4x + 2.80(12 - x) = 42.00 \rightarrow 4x + 33.60 - 2.80x = 42.00 \rightarrow 1.20x = 8.40 \rightarrow x = 7$

Thus, the answer is (D).

16. **(C)**

From statement (1) you know that the amount of gasoline in the tank is $\frac{2}{3}$ of the tank's capacity, but you do not know the tank's capacity, and so (1) alone is insufficient. Thus, the answer is (B), (C) or (E). From the statement (2) you know only that the amount of gasoline in the tank is 0.75 kiloliters less than the tank's capacity, and so (2) alone is insufficient. Therefore, the answer is (C) or (E). If the capacity of tank is x kiloliters, then (1) and (2) together imply that $x - 0.75 = \frac{2}{3}x$, or $x = 2.25$ kiloliters. Thus there are 1.5 kiloliters of gasoline in the tank and the answer is C.

17. **(D)**

Representing the number of crackers Missy ate as M, and the number that Audrey ate as A, we can write an algebraic expression to represent the first portion of the question as: $M = m + A$ (1). Knowing that the combined number of crackers they ate ($M + A$) was equal to the total number originally in the box (n) gives us the second formula: $M + A = n$, or $A = n - M$ (2). By substituting equation (2) into equation (1), we get: $M = m + (n - M)$, then we solve for M. This can be reduced to $2M = m + n$ (consolidating all of the Ms). Then you can get $M = \frac{(m + n)}{2}$ by dividing the coefficient next to the variable. This question could also be solved by the addition/subtraction method. Regardless of the method used, the answer is (D).

18. **(C)**

If Jenna's age now = J, then $J + 14 = 48 \rightarrow J = 48 - 14$, or 34. Jenna's age x years ago is equal to $34 - x$. The correct answer is (C).

19. **(B)**

This is a perfect example of keeping track of units. We want an answer in "hours" and we have two facts stated in "miles" and "miles/hour." So divide "miles" by "miles/hour" to get an answer with the units "hours," as shown: $\dfrac{y \text{ miles}}{(x \text{ miles/hour})} = \left(\dfrac{y}{x}\right)$ hours.

20. **(C)**

If w is the number of women in the room and m is the number of men in the room, then the question is: what is the value of $m - w$? Statement (1) says that $w + m = 20$, which is not sufficient to answer the question, so the answer must be (B), (C), or (E). Statement (2) says that $m = w^2$, which has several solutions: e.g. $m = 4$, $w = 2$, $m = 9$, or $w = 3$. These cases would give different answers to the value of $m - w$. So, statement (2) is not sufficient to answer the question. However, if both statements are used then $w + m = 20 = w + w^2$. Therefore, $w^2 + w - 20 = 0$

$$(w + 5)(w - 4) = 0$$

$$w = -5; w = 4$$

Thus, the two statements together yield a single positive solution, $w = 4$, which means that $m = 16$ and $m - w +12$. Therefore, both statements together are sufficient to answer the question, and the answer is (C).

21. **(C)**

If you let the number of female employees in Company X be f and the number of male

employees be m, then according to statement (1), if 14 females are hired, the ratio of males to females can be expressed as $\frac{m}{f+14}$, which equals $\frac{16}{9}$. Since the equation has two unknowns, it is not sufficient to determine the value of f, and the answer is (B), (C), or (E). Statement (2) tells you that $m = f + 105$. Again, this equation involves two unknowns and is not sufficient alone to determine the value of f. However if the two equations are used together, f can be determined. Substituting $f + 105$ for m in the first equation yields the progression below.

$\frac{f+105}{f+14} = \frac{16}{9}$

$16f + 224 = 9f + 945$

$7f = 721$

$f = 103$

Thus both statements together are necessary and the answer is (C).

22. **(A)**

From (1), it can be determined that F did not receive the most votes since G and H received the remaining 29 votes, and G and H could not both have received less than 11 votes. Thus, from (1) alone it can be determined whether or not F received the most votes, and the answer must be (A) or (D). From (2), it can only be determined that F and G received 26 votes combined; however, F may or may not have received more than 14 votes. Therefore, the answer is (A).

23. **(D)**

From the first sentence, we know that $X + Y = 1600$ (1)

From the second, we know that $x = 3.Y - 100$ (2)

This problem can be solved either by substitution, or by combining two linear equations.

By substitution: (1) $y = 1600 - X$; (2) $100 + X = 3.(1600 - X)$

$100 + x = 4800 - 3X$

$4X = 4700$

$X = 1175$

By combining the linear equations:

(1) $x + y = 1600$

(2) $x - 3Y = -100$

Subtracting (2) from (1) gives:

$4Y = 1700 \rightarrow y = 425$

$X = 1600 - y = 1600 - 425 = 1175$.

No matter how you do it, the correct answer is (D).

24. **(A)**

This is a rate problem, except here the quantity, rather than distance or amount of work, is the number of hot dogs; if John takes 12 minutes to eat x hot dogs ($\frac{12}{x}$ min/dog), then we can multiply that by the number of seconds in a minute to determine how many seconds per dog: $\frac{12}{x} \frac{\text{min}}{\text{dog}} \cdot \frac{60 \text{ sec}}{1 \text{ min}} = 12 \cdot \frac{60}{x} \frac{\text{sec}}{\text{dog}} \cdot \frac{1 \text{ min}}{1 \text{ min}} = \frac{720}{x} \frac{\text{sec}}{\text{dog}}$. In order to determine how many seconds it will take John to eat z dogs, we now multiply the previous expression by z. Notice in both operations above and below how the units cancel similarly to common factors in a fraction.

$\frac{720}{x} \frac{\text{sec}}{\text{dog}} \cdot z \text{ dog} = \frac{720 \cdot z}{x} \text{ sec} \cdot \frac{\text{dog}}{\text{dog}} = \frac{720z}{x} \text{ sec} \cdot \frac{\text{dog}}{\text{dog}} = \frac{720z}{x} \text{ sec}$

The correct answer is (A).

25. **(B)**

Saying that $w > x$ means that we know that x is to the left of w on the number line (but we don't know how far): $x\text{------------}w$. "y is the midpoint between w and z" means that those three letters occur in on of the following orders: $z\text{---}y\text{---}w$ or $w\text{---}y\text{---}z$. Because x must be twice as far from z as it is from w, we know that the configuration of the four letters must look like one of the the following (drawn roughly to scale): $z\text{---}y\text{-}x\text{--}w$ or $x\text{--}w\text{-}y\text{-}z$. In the first scenario, $\frac{w-y}{z-x} = \frac{3}{-4} = -\frac{3}{4}$. This is not one of the answer choices, so we must try the second senario. In this scenario, $\frac{w-y}{z-x} = \frac{-1}{4} = -\frac{1}{4}$. The answer is (B). Note that if you had tried the

second scenario first, you could have stopped after finding $-\frac{1}{4}$, because the question asks what the expression *could* equal.

26. **(B)**

Statement (1) is not sufficient since it implies only that the bucket will hold at least 9 liters. Therefore, the answer must be (B), (C) or (E). With respect to statement (2), if c is the capacity of Marcia's bucket and the addition of 3 liters of water increases the volume of the water from $\frac{1}{2}c$ to $\frac{4}{3}(\frac{1}{2}c) - \frac{1}{2}c = 3$, then $\frac{4}{3}(\frac{1}{2})c - \frac{1}{2}c = 3$ which can be solved for c. The answer is (B).

27. **(D)**

The first step gives you $x \cdot \frac{3}{5} = \frac{3x}{5}$

The second step gives you $\sqrt{\frac{3x}{5}} = x$;

Square both sides of the equation to get $\frac{3x}{5} = x^2$

Isolate all terms with x on the left side: $-x^2 + \frac{3x}{5} = 0$

Factor out $-x$: $-x(x - \frac{3}{5}) = 0$. Because we know x cannot equal 0, x must equal $\frac{3}{5}$.

28. **(C)**

If F is the height of the first building and S is the initial height of the second, we know from the problem that: $F + S = x$ and $F = S + 37$. By substituting the second equation into the first we get: $(S + 37) + S = x$; solving for x gives, $S = \frac{(x - 37)}{2}$. Adding an antenna to the second building will give it a total (new) height of: $S + z = \frac{(x - 37)}{2} + z$.

29. **(B)**

Statement (1) alone is clearly insufficient to answer the question because no relationship between the driving speeds of Rhodes and Smith is given. Thus, The correct answer must be (B), (C) or (E). From statement (2) you know that Rhodes' average driving speed was $\frac{140}{2}$ or 70 kilometers per hour. Therefore, the answer is (B).

30. **(B)**

If the number of men employed at Company X is m and the number of women is w,

then from (1) the ratio of the number of technicians to the total number of employees

is $\frac{0.04m + 0.55w}{m + w}$. Since you do not know any relationship between m and w, (1) alone is in

sufficient. For example, if $m = w$, then 47.5 percent of employees are technicians; but if w

$+ 2m$, then 50 percent of the employees are technicians. Thus, the answer is (B), (C), or (E).

Statement (2) implies that $\frac{9}{20}$, or 45 percent, of the employees are technicians. Therefore,

the answer is (B).

31. **(A)**

From (1) and the information given in the problem, it can be determined that

$\frac{\text{Sue's Distance}}{\text{Sue's Time } t} = \frac{\text{Bill's Distance } d}{3t}$ or $\frac{10}{t} = \frac{d}{3t}$ and $d = 30$ kilometers. Therefore, the answer

must be (A) or (D). Since (2) gives no information about Sue's time (from which we could

compute Bill's time) and Bill's speed, the question cannot be answered from (2) alone and

the answer is (A).

32. **(B)**

In this problem, two equations are given, and we are told that the two equations are equal

to each other (since $x = y$). Using this information, one must solve for k. $x = 5 - 4k$ and

$y = 5k - 3 \rightarrow x = y = 5 - 4k = 5k - 3$. $5 - 4k = 5k - 3$ can be solved by isolating the variable.

This can be done in two simple steps: Adding $4k$ to both sides and adding 3 to both sides.

Step 1: $(+ 4k) + 5 - 4k = 5k - 3 + (+ 4k) \rightarrow 5 = 9k - 3$

Step 2: $(+3) + 5 = 9k - 3 + (+3) \rightarrow 8 = 9k$

To solve the final equation, both sides should be divided by 9 in the following manner:

$\frac{8}{9} = \frac{9k}{9} \rightarrow \frac{8}{9} = k$ Therefore, $\frac{8}{9}$ is the solution, and (B) is the correct answer.

33. **(D)**

We can rewrite $(5^k)^{7/3}$ as $5^{7k/3}$ and 25 as 5^2, so that the equation now reads: $5^{7k/3} = 5^2$.

Because the base of each expression is the same, and the two expressions are equal, the exponents also must equal one another. i.e: $\frac{7k}{3} = 2$. By multiplying both sides of the equations by $\frac{3}{7}$, we get $k = \frac{6}{7}$, and the correct answer is (D).

34. **(B)**

$4^3 = 64$; $5^3 = 125$. Because 115 falls between 64 and 125, x must be between 4 and 5 and the correct answer is (B).

35. **(A)**

Since $(2^x)(2^y) = 8$ can be written as $2^{x+y} = 2^3$, it follows, by equating exponents, that $x + y = 3$. Similarly, $(9^x)(3^y) = 81$ can be written as $3^{2x+y} = 3^4 \rightarrow 2x + y = 4$. Therefore, from the first equation $y = 3 - x$. Substituting for y into the second equation gives the following: $2x + 3-x = 4$, or $x = 1$. Therefore, $y = 2$ and $(x, y) = (1, 2)$. Thus, the answer is (A).

36. **(B)**

In order to solve this problem, it is necessary to manipulate the left side of the equation until it is in the same form as the right hand side.

$$\frac{0.0024 \cdot 10^j}{0.08 \cdot 10^r} = \frac{0.0024 \cdot 10^j}{0.0008 \cdot 10^2 \cdot 10^r} = \frac{0.0024}{0.0008} \cdot \frac{10^j}{10^{r+2}} = 3 \cdot 10^{j-r-2} = 3 \cdot 10^6$$

So: $j - r - 2 = 6$; adding 2 to both sides gives $j - r = 8$, and the correct answer is (B).

37. **(D)**

The goal in these problems is to make the bases of each side of the equation look identical so that you can equate the exponents. In this problem, that does not seem possible until you start manipulating algebraically. On the left side of the equation it is possible to factor out 3^x from $3^x - 3^{(x-1)}$. The result is this: $3x(1 - 3^{-1})$ which is the same as $3^x(1 - \frac{1}{3})$ which is the same as $3^x(\frac{2}{3})$. Multiplying both sides of the equation by 3 you see that $3^x 2 = 3^{14} 2$ and $x = 14$. The faster solution is to recognize that you should be factoring out 3^{x-1} (it is smaller than 3^x). You end up with $3^{x-1}(3-1) = 3^{13} 2$ which is $3^{x-1} 2 = 3^{13} 2$ and $x - 1 = 13$. Therefore $x = 14$.

38. (C)

The expression can be rewritten as: $2n = n^2$; subtracting $2n$ from both sides gives: $n^2 - 2n = 0$. Factoring yields $n(n - 2) = 0$, so n can be equal to either 2 or 0. The correct answer is (C).

39. (E)

Statement (1) suggests that n could be 4, 9, 16, 25, 36, 49, 64, or 81, thus Statement (1) is insufficient. Statement (2) would let n be 16 or 81 and is also insufficient alone. Both statements are satisfied by the numbers 16 and 81 so even together there is insufficient information to determine the value of n. The correct answer is (E).

40. (E)

This process requires comprehensive knowledge of properties of exponents in order to simplify the expression. First, change all the negative exponents by switching the variable from the numerator to the denominator, or vice versa, as in the following example: $x^5 = \frac{1}{x^5}$
Next, expand the figures in the parentheses as follows: $(x^4)^2 = x^8$; $(x^{-5})^4 = x^{-20}$. Then, add the exponents for the following expression: $\frac{(x^8)(x^3)(x^7)(x^{20})}{(x)(x^5)}$. It becomes $\frac{x^{38}}{x^6} = x^{32}$. Therefore, (E) is the correct answer choice.

41. (B)

By substituting 5^{25} for x, $(5^{25})^{5^{25}} = 5^k$. Using the third exponent rule relating to parentheses, we know that the left side of the equation looks like this after multiplying our two exponents: $5^{25 \cdot 5^{25}}$ By manipulating the 25 we can simplify further to $5^{5^2 \cdot 5^{25}}$ which equals $5^{5^{27}}$. The manipulated equation now looks like this: $5^{5^{27}} = 5^k$ and because we have like bases on each side of the equal sign, we know that $k = 5^{27}$.

42. (D)

Changing to exponents we see that this is $\left(\left(\left((512)^{\frac{1}{3}}\right)^{\frac{1}{2}}\right)^{\frac{1}{3}}\right)^2$ which $= 512^{\frac{1}{3} \cdot \frac{1}{2} \cdot \frac{1}{3} \cdot 2} = 512^{\frac{1}{9}} = \sqrt[9]{512}$.

From the Arithmetic Lesson you can recognize that $2^9 = 512$, so the answer is 2.

43. **(D)**

If $x^y = x^{2y-3}$, then $y = 2y - 3$, and $y = 3$. To determine x^y, or x^3, one only needs the value of x.

Statement (1) gives the value of x, and the value of x can be found from statement (2).

Thus, the answer is (D).

44. **(A)**

Multiplying each side by $5^{1/x}$,

$5^{1/x}(5\sqrt[x]{125}) = 1 \rightarrow 5^{1/x}(\sqrt[x]{125}) = \frac{1}{5}$

Since $125 = 5^3$, $5^{1/x}(\sqrt[x]{5^3}) = \frac{1}{5} \rightarrow 5^{1/x}(5^{3/x}) = \frac{1}{5}$

This can be simplified to $5^{4/x} = \frac{1}{5}$

$\frac{1}{5} = 5^{-1}$ so $5^{4/x}$ can be equated to 5^{-1}.

Therefore, since $5^{4/x} = 5^{-1}$, $\frac{4}{x} = -1$, and $x = -4$

Thus, answer choice (A) is the correct answer.

45. **(C)**

Anytime you have decimals with exponents or under the root sign, it is a good idea to convert them to fractions. The first step here is to replace the decimals with fractions and remove the negative exponents by flipping their locations to produce the following:

$$\frac{(\frac{4}{100})^3}{(\frac{8}{100})^4} = \frac{\frac{4^3}{100^3}}{\frac{8^4}{100^4}}$$

Next step is to remove the fraction in the denominator by multiplying the top and bottom by its reciprocal. This results in $\frac{4^3}{100^3} \cdot \frac{100^4}{8^4} = \frac{4^3 \cdot 100}{8^4}$.

Simplifying further: $\frac{2^6 \cdot 100}{2^{12}} = \frac{100}{2^6} = \frac{100}{64} = \frac{25}{16}$.

46. (C)

Since $(-2)^{2m} = ((-2)^2)^m = 4^m = 2^{2m}$, it follows that $2^{2m} = 2^{9-m}$. The exponents must be equal, so that $2m = 9 - m$, or $m = 3$. The answer is (C).

47. (A)

Solve the first equation for x. $x = 6x + 6y$ and $-5x = 6y$, so $x = -\frac{6}{5}y$. Substituting in the second expression, you see that $\dfrac{y}{y - \frac{6}{5}y} = \dfrac{y}{\frac{-1}{5}y} = -5$. Picking numbers is also very effective in this problem. Choose numbers that will satisfy the initial equation and then plug them in to get the value of the second example. For instance, try $x = 6$ and $y = -5$. Plugging them in, you quickly get the correct answer of -5.

48. (B)

This problem requires some tricky algebraic manipulation. First, multiply both sides of the equation by the denominator of the fraction: $(0.25 + x)$. This results in the following equation: $(0.25 + x) \cdot \dfrac{3.5}{0.25 + x} = 10 \cdot (0.25 + x) \rightarrow 3.5 = 10\,(0.25 + x)$. Next, use the distributive property of multiplication and multiply each figure in the parentheses by the number outside the parenthesis (10): $3.5 = (10 \cdot 0.25) + (10x)$. Simplify the equation: $3.5 = 2.5 + 10x$. Isolate the variable on one side of the equation by subtracting 2.5 from both sides: $3.5 - 2.5 = 2.5 + 10x - 2.5 \rightarrow 1 = 10x$. From there, divide both sides by 10: $\dfrac{1}{10} = \dfrac{10x}{10} \rightarrow \dfrac{1}{10} = x$. Therefore, 0.1 is the answer, and answer choice (B) is the correct answer.

49. (B)

First, a common denominator must be found; 30 works well. Then the equation can be transformed into the following: $\dfrac{6 \cdot 2(x-2)}{6 \cdot 5} + \dfrac{5 \cdot (24 - 12x)}{5 \cdot 6} + \dfrac{30 \cdot 2x}{30} = \dfrac{6 \cdot 4x}{6 \cdot 5} + \dfrac{30 \cdot 3}{30}$

This can then be simplified to:

$\dfrac{12(x-2)}{30} + \dfrac{5(24 - 12x)}{30} + \dfrac{60x}{30} = \dfrac{24x}{30} + \dfrac{90}{30} \rightarrow \dfrac{12x - 24}{30} + \dfrac{120 - 60x}{30} + \dfrac{60x}{30} = \dfrac{24x}{30} + \dfrac{90}{30}$

Now the denominator, since it is the same in all cases, can be removed by multiplying everything by 30: $(12x - 24) + (120 - 60x) + 60x = 24x + 90$. This can be simplified to: $12x + 96 = 24x + 90 \rightarrow 12x = 6 \rightarrow x = \frac{1}{2}$. Therefore, answer choice (B) is the correct answer.

50. **(C)**

Multiplying both sides of the fraction, $\frac{4 - x}{2 + x} = x$ by $2 + x$ yields the following:

$4 - x = x(2 + x) = 2x + x^2$, or $x^2 + 3x - 4 = 0$. Thus, the value of $x^2 + 3x - 4$ is 0, and the answer is (C).

51. **(C)**

First, the numbers inside the parentheses need to be simplified: $(\sqrt{11} + \sqrt{11} + \sqrt{11}) = 3\sqrt{11}$

To square, 3 should be squared, and $\sqrt{11}$ should also be squared. Therefore,

$(3\sqrt{11})^2 = 3^2 \cdot \sqrt{11}^2 \rightarrow 9 \times 11 = 99$. The answer is thus (C).

52. **(A)**

When working with three equations and three unknowns, set a goal of eliminating the same variable using two different combinations of equations. This will yield 2 equations and 2 unknowns. Since we want to solve for z, it would be best not to eliminate it. Let's start by eliminating x. If we set up the first two equations given as simultaneous equations, and add them together, they should appear as follows:

$-3y + x - 10z = 67$

$\underline{2y - x + 5z = -17}$

$-y \qquad -5z = 50$

Then eliminate x again by using a different set of equations. Multiply the second equation given by two, and subtract the third equation given from the resulting equation.

$(2y - x + 5z = -17)2 = 4y - 2x + 10z = -34$

$$\underline{-y - 2x + 5z = 100}$$

$$5y + 5z = -134$$

Now we have two equations and two unknowns. To eliminate y and be left with z, multiply the first equation you simplified by 5 and add it to the second as follows:

$(-y - 5z = 50)5 = -5y - 25z = 250$

$$\underline{5y + 5z = -134}$$

$$-20z = 116 \qquad z = -\frac{116}{20} = -\frac{29}{5} \text{ (A)}$$

53. (D)

In order to solve for k, begin by multiplying the entire equation through by k to get:

$z^2 + 4zk + 3k = z$. Then, isolate the terms with k on the left side and those without k on the right: $4zk + 3k = z - z^2$. Then, factor k out of the terms on the left side: $k(4z + 3) = z - z^2$. Finally, divide both sides by the "coefficient" for k (which in this case is made up of z terms):

$k = \frac{(z - z2)}{(4z + 3)}$. So, the correct answer is (D). Alternatively, one could plug in numbers for z to determine the solution.

54. (D)

Substitution can be used to solve for the variables in these two equations. First, substitute the first equation into the second: $x = 3 - (17x + 32) + 2x$. When simplified, this becomes the following: $x = -29 - 15x \rightarrow 16x = -29 \rightarrow x = -\frac{29}{16}$. Use this figure to solve for y, by substituting it back into the first equation: $y = 17 (-\frac{29}{16}) + 32$. By forming a common denominator, this can be simplified into a fraction, as given in the answer choices:

$y = -\frac{493}{16} + \frac{32 \cdot 16}{16} = -\frac{493}{16} + \frac{512}{16}$. The numerators should be summed: $-493 + 512 = 19$.

Thus, $y = \frac{19}{16}$, and answer choice (D) is the correct answer.

55. **(C)**

Using the given information, $(b - 3)(4 + \frac{2}{b}) = 0$, it follows that one of the factors equals 0. So, either $b - 3 = 0$ or $4 + \frac{2}{b} = 0$. Solving for b, that means that either $b = 3$ or $b = -\frac{1}{2}$. But $b \neq 3$ is given, so $b = -\frac{1}{2}$, and the answer is (C).

56. **(D)**

Each answer choice must be assessed separately. (A): This answer is obtained by adding 4 to both sides of the equation $25x^2 = y^2 - 4$. (B): This answer is obtained by multiplying both sides of the original equation by 3. (C): This answer is equivalent because $y^2 - 4 = (y + 2)(y - 2)$. (E): This answer is obtained by dividing both sides of the original equation by 25. By the process of elimination, the answer must be (D). Squaring both sides of (D), $5x = y - 2$, gives the following: $25x^2 = y^2 - 4y + 4$, which is NOT equivalent to the original equation. Therefore, the answer is (D).

57. **(D)**

With respect to statement (1), since x, y, and z are positive, both sides of the equation can be multiplied by $\frac{x}{z}$ to produce the identical equation $x = \frac{y}{z^2}$. Thus, the answer must be (A) or (D). Statement (2) is also an equivalent equation, which can be seen by squaring both sides of the equation and then solving for x. Since each statement gives sufficient information, the answer is (D).

58. **(C)**

-1 raised to any even power (2, 4, etc.) is equal to 1. -1 raised to any odd power (1, 3, 5) is equal to -1. Plugging in to the expression gives: $- (1 - 1 + 1 - 1) = -0 = 0$. So, the correct answer is (C).

59. **(B)**

The (+1) is irrelevant in very large values of x, e.g. 5,999. So, the fraction can be best estimated as if the (+1) did not exist: $\frac{2x}{5x} = \frac{2}{5}$. Therefore, answer (B) is the best choice.

60. (C)

The choices can be compared quickly, as follows: The first choice is $\frac{1}{0.2} = 5$. The second choice is $(0.2)^2 = 0.04$. The third choice is 0.02. The fourth choice is $\frac{0.2}{2} = 0.1$. The fifth choice is 0.2. Therefore, the smallest number is 0.02; thus, answer choice (C) is the correct answer.

61. (A)

It may be helpful first to simplify the given equation.

$$S = \frac{\frac{2}{n}}{\frac{1}{x} + \frac{2}{3x}} = \frac{\frac{2}{n}}{\frac{3}{3x} + \frac{2}{3x}} = \frac{\frac{2}{n}}{\frac{5}{3x}} = \frac{2}{n}\left(\frac{3x}{5}\right) = \frac{6x}{5\left(\frac{1}{2}\right)}$$

Substituting $x = 2n$ from statement (1) gives $S = \frac{6(2n)}{5n} = \frac{12}{5}$. Thus, (1) alone is sufficient, and the answer must be (A) or (D). Statement (2) alone is not sufficient, since substituting $n = \frac{1}{2}$ gives $S = \frac{6x}{5n}$, and the value of S cannot be determined unless the value of x is known. The answer is (A).

62. (D)

From statement (1), $2^{\sqrt{x}} = 8 = 2^3$ Thus, $\sqrt{x} = 3$, which implies that $x = 9$. Since 2^9 is greater than 100, statement (1) alone is sufficient to answer the question, and the answer is (A) or (D). From statement (2), $\frac{1}{2^x} < 0.01$ implies that $2^x > \frac{1}{0.01}$, or $2^x > 100$, which is sufficient to answer the question. Therefore, each statement alone is sufficient to answer the question, and the answer is (D).

63. (B)

We know that $x^3 = xy$ and x cannot equal 0. Subtracting xy from each side gives: $x^3 - xy = 0$.

Factoring out x yields: $x(x^2 - y) = 0$. Because x cannot equal 0, $x^2 - y$ must equal 0. Therefore $x^2 = y$, and the correct answer is (B).

64. **(D)**

All numbers have a repeating pattern of units digits when raised to certain exponents. The Units Digit chart from the Arithmetic lesson shows this pattern and it is important for many difficult number properties questions. While you do not need to memorize this chart, it is important that you know it exists and that you are always able to determine the units digit of any integer taken to any power. In this case, the units digit of powers of 2 has a repeating pattern of 2, 4, 8, and 6 before going back to 2. That is, the pattern repeats every 4th power. 4 goes into 39 nine times with a remainder of 3. Therefore the unit's digit of 2^{36} is 6 and the unit's digit of 2^{39} is 8.

65. **(C)**

This is another difficult number property question testing your understanding of factors. First, rephrase the question in simple language. By asking for p, the question is really asking how many 10s can divide into the number m, which is the product of all numbers from 1 to 40. Or put another way, how many 10s are contained in 40? (m is the product of all numbers from 1 to 40 which can be denoted as 40 factorial – $(1 \cdot 2 \cdot 3 \cdot 4 \cdot 5 \ldots .40)$. As the number 10 is made up of $2 \cdot 5$, you need to determine how many pairings of 2 and 5 there are in 40! Because there are so many more 2s contained in the number m than 5s, the number of 5s will determine the number of 10s (pairings of $2 \cdot 5$) that exist. So simply march up the number line and count any number that has 5 as a factor – (5, 10, 15, 20, 25, 30, 35, 40). There are eight numbers that have 5 as a factor. However, the answer is not 8 because 25 is a perfect square of 5 so its prime factorization contains two 5s not just one. Therefore there are 9 of the number 10 (pairings of 5 and 2) in the number m, and the answer is (C).

66. **(D)**

To answer this question, you must first determine the units digit of each individual number in the subtraction calculation. This is done using your knowledge of the repeating patterns that exist for all units digits raised to certain exponents. 7^{15} must end in 3 because of the same repeating pattern (for 7 it is 7 , 9, 3, 1, 7, 9, 3, 1, etc.) that exists for every units digit as outlined in the chart. Once you know what the numbers look like, you can determine the units digit of this subtraction by using your understanding of this basic arithmetic operation. 9^{19} has a units digit of 9 because numbers ending in 9 raised to an odd exponent will always end in 9. As the top number ends in 9 and the bottom number ends in 3, and we know that the top number is larger than the bottom, the result will be 9 - 3 = 6. As a result the answer is (D).

9^{19} XXXXXXXXX9

7^{15} <u>- XXXXXXXX3</u>

           XXXXXXXXX6

67. **(C)**

Similar to question 53, this question deals with the sum of digits within a number. Because 10^{30} is a 1 with 30 zeros after it, when you subtract 37 from it, the result is going to be a number that looks like this: 999999…..99963. Just imagine the subtraction calculation:

10000…..00000

<u>- 37</u>

 9999…..99963

That end result shown above will have exactly the same number of digits as the number of zeros: 30. To determine the sum of the digits of this number, we need to sum up all the 9s plus the 6 and the 3. We know that the result of this subtraction number contains 30 digits so there must be 28 9s and the 6 and the 3. To determine this sum, it is easiest to realize that 6 + 3 = 9 so you are really asking for the product of 29 · 9. As this product must end in 1, (C) is the correct answer.

68. **(C)**

Statement (1) alone is not sufficient, for if $n^4 < 25$, then $n = 1$ or $n = 2$, since $1^4 = 1$ and $2^4 = 16$. Therefore, the answer must be (B), (C), or (E). Statement (2) implies only that n is not equal to 1. Statements (1) and (2) together are sufficient, since eliminating $n = 1$ leaves $n = 2$. The answer is (C).

69. **(B)**

Statement (1) is insufficient to determine whether $x > y$ because all it tells us is that $|x| > |y|$. For example, if $x = 3$ and $y = 2$, $x > y$, but if $x = -3$ and $y = 2$, $x < y$. However, we can add y to both sides of Statement (2) to obtain $x > y$. Thus, Statement (2) is sufficient, and the answer is (B).

70. **(D)**

In order to determine the units digit of a product, it is only necessary to multiply the units digits of the factors. For example the units digit of $123 \cdot 456$ can be found by multiplying $3 \cdot 6 = 18$, and taking the units digit of that (8). Equivalently, when determining the units digit of 23^6 it is only necessary to find the units digit for $3^6 = 3 \cdot 3 \cdot 3 \cdot 3 \cdot 3 \cdot 3 = (3 \cdot 3) \cdot (3 \cdot 3) \cdot (3 \cdot 3) = 9 \cdot 9 \cdot 9 = 81 \cdot 9 \rightarrow$ so the units digit of the whole sequence 23^6 is $81 \cdot 9 = 9$. Through a similar methodology, the units digit of 17^3 is the same as the units digit of 7^3 which is equal to 3. The units digit of 61^9 is equal to 1^9, or 1. Multiplying the three units digits (9, 3, and 1) together gives the answer 27, which has a units digit of 7. So the correct answer is (D).

71. **(C)**

If $x = 0$, then y must equal 10, since $x + y = 10$. 10 is the minimum possible value for $x + y$, and can also occur when $x = 10$ and $y = 0$. Because the minima occur when x and y are as different from one another as possible, we can infer that the maximum occurs when $x = y$. Plugging in x for y in the original equation $x^2 + x^2 = 2x^2 = 100$, or $x^2 = 50$. Because we know that $7^2 = 49$, we know that x must be just slightly larger than 7. $x = y$, so y must also be slightly larger than 7; therefore, $x + y$ is slightly larger than 14, and the correct answer is (C).

72. **(A)**

This problem can be solved without any calculations, just by looking at the answer choices. Three things must be understood. First, if x is positive, then $\frac{x^3}{27}$ will become a large positive number that will subsequently be made negative by the negative sign in front of $\frac{x^3}{27}$. Therefore, a positive number will yield a small value for y, because it will be below 0. Secondly, 0 will yield a value of 0, which is not very high. Thirdly, the larger the number (in an absolute sense), the greater the value of $\frac{x^3}{27}$, based on the property of an exponent greater than 1. From these three properties, it can be determined that $x > 0$, and should be as high as possible in absolute value. Thus, -27 fits this criterion best, and answer choice (A) is the correct answer choice.

73. **(C)**

This is another problem focusing on your understanding of factoring. In this question, you are trying to determine if xy is divisible by 9 (in other words whether it contains the necessary 3^2 in its prime factorization). From the 1st statement it is unclear whether xy is divisible by 9. Consider a few possibilities – if xy is equal to 12 then it is divisible by 6 as required in the 1st statement but it is not divisible by 9. However, if xy is equal to 18 then it is divisible by 6 and 9. The end result is that the answer could be yes or no from this information so statement 1 is insufficient. Statement 2 alone is clearly insufficient as x and y could be any perfect squares. Together, however you are certain that xy will be divisible by 9. If the product of x and y is divisible by 6 then there must a 3 and a 2 in its prime factorization. If, however, x and y are each perfect squares then it is impossible to only have one 2 and one 3. At a minimum there must be a 2^2 and a 3^2 in the prime factorization of the product xy. As a result that product will always be divisible by 9. Answer is (C).

74. **(C)**

it is understood that an odd number times an even number yields an even number. Only an odd number times another odd number can yield an odd product. Therefore, the value of y must be 0, so that $4^0 = 1$. From there, the equation becomes: $3^x(1) = 177,147$, and since $y = 0$, and $x - y = 11$, it can be determined that $x - 0 = 11$ or $x = 11$. Therefore, answer choice (C) is the correct answer.

75. **(A)**

$\sqrt{x^2y^2}$ is equal to the $\sqrt{x^2} \cdot \sqrt{y^2}$ so let's look at each calculation individually. Because the radical sign denotes the positive square root of a number we know that $\sqrt{x^2} = |x|$ and $\sqrt{y^2} = |y|$. The correct answer must be equal to $|x| \cdot |y|$ which will always be positive. Because x is given as negative, we need to choose $-xy$ to give us a positive result and the answer is (A). If you are confused here simply consider some numbers. If $x = -3$ (x is defined as less than 0 in this question) then $x^2 = 9$ and the $\sqrt{9} = 3$. If $y = 5$ (y is defined as greater than 0 in the question) then $y^2 = 25$ and $\sqrt{25} = 5$. So using our picked numbers the answer is 15. Looking at our answer choices we need to plug back in our values for x and y and find one that is equivalent to positive 15. Answer choice A gives us $- (-3)(5)$ which equals 15 so (A) is correct. (B), (C), and (D) all give us the answer of -15 which is not correct. Because x^2y^2 will always be positive there will always be a solution and (E) is wrong.

76. **(E)**

In approaching a question such as this, you should remember to consider the possibility of negative values of x and y. Note that $y < y + 1$ for all values of y, so that $\frac{1}{y} > \frac{1}{y+1}$ for $y > 0$ or for $y < -1$, whereas $\frac{1}{y} < \frac{1}{y+1}$ for $-1 < x < 0$. Thus, if $x > y > 0$, then $\frac{x}{y} > \frac{x}{y+1}$, but if $y < x < -1$, then $\frac{x}{y} < \frac{x}{y+1}$. Therefore, the order relation between $\frac{x}{y}$ and $\frac{x}{y+1}$ cannot be determined from (1) and (2) together. The answer is (E).

77. **(E)**

This number property question combines your understanding of odd-even properties and factors. The question is asking for a definitive conclusion that can be made about the product of any three consecutive positive integers $(n)(n + 1)(n + 2)$. Consider each answer choice individually. (A): This product will always be even because three consecutive integers always contain at least one even number. The product of an even number with any other number(s) will always be even. Therefore (A) is incorrect as it does not matter if n is even or odd. (B): For the same reason as in (A), (B) is incorrect. (C): This product can never be odd for the reasons discussed in (A) and (B). (D): This product will always be divisible by 3. Three consecutive numbers must contain a multiple of 3. Pick any three numbers along the number line and you will see this to be true (7, 8, 9, 15, 16, 17, 31, 32, 33). Therefore, (D) is incorrect because it does not matter whether n is odd or even – the product will always be divisible by 3. (E): By process of elimination, you can pick (E) but it is important that you understand why this must be true. If n is even then $(n + 2)$ must also be even. In this scenario, the product of $n(n + 1)(n + 2)$ must always be divisible by 4 because the product contains two even numbers. (Any number that results from multiplying 2 even numbers is always divisible by 4). As mentioned above, the product of three consecutive numbers is always divisible by 3. Therefore, in this scenario, the product of $n(n + 1)(n + 2)$ must contain both a 3 and a 4. The product of 3 and 4 is 12 so this number will always be divisible by 12.

78. **(B)**

First, factor the original equation: $x^2 - 7x + 12 = (x - 4)(x - 3) = 0$. This shows us that the two roots are 3 and 4. Then determine if any of the answer choices have the same roots (through factoring), or plug in 3 and 4 for x in each answer choice. (A): This answer is unfactorable (i.e. no real roots). (B): This answer is factored as $(x - 4)(x + 3)$, with roots 4, and -3, so it has 1 root in common with the original equation. (C): This equation does not factor into integers, so neither root is 4 or 3. (D): If you divide through by 3 to get $x^2 - 3 = 0$, you can factor the resulting equation into $(x - \sqrt{3})(x + \sqrt{3})$; the roots are $\sqrt{3}$ and $-\sqrt{3}$. (E):

This equation is factored as $(x + 3)(x - 2)$ with roots of -3 and 2. The correct answer is (B), because both the equation in B and that in the question have a common root of 4.

79. **(D)**

In order to solve this problem, the factored expression must be expanded.

$(x - 5)^2 = x^2 - 10x + 25$

This information can be equated to the expression with the variable, y.

$x^2 - 10x + 25 = x^2 - \frac{xy}{5} + 25$

The majority of the equation is the same and can be cancelled out, leaving: $-10x = -\frac{xy}{5}$.

Solving for y yields $y = 50$. Therefore, answer choice (D) is the correct answer.

80. **(E)**

To solve for x, this problem must be factored. However, when attempting to solve this, one comes up with the following: $(3x - \_) \cdot (x - \_)$ where the two blanks must be 1 and 3. The two options would thus be: $(3x - 1) \cdot (x - 3) = 3x^2 - 10x + 3$ Answers: $x = \frac{1}{3}, 3$

$(3x - 3) \cdot (x - 1) = 3x^2 - 6x + 3$ Answer: $x = 1$

Neither option matches the given equation or any of the answer choices.

For clarification, one should use the quadratic equation: $\frac{-b \pm \sqrt{b^2 - 4ac}}{2a}$ where the expression under the radical must be positive in order for a real answer to exist.

$b^2 - 4ac$, in this case, is $(-5)^2 - 4(3)(3) = 25 - 36 = -11$

Therefore, there are no solutions, and (E) is the correct answer.

81. **(C)**

The expression $x^2 - y^2$ is a positive number if, and only if, both of its factors $(x + y)$ and $(x - y)$ have the same sign. Since both (1) and (2) are needed to establish that the two factors have the same sign, the answer is (C).

82. **(D)**

To remove the roots from the denominator in this problem you must recognize the need to use the difference of squares. By multiplying the top and bottom of the expression by $\sqrt{x+1} - \sqrt{x}$ you get the following: $\dfrac{\sqrt{x+1} - \sqrt{x}}{(\sqrt{x+1} + \sqrt{x})(\sqrt{x+1} - \sqrt{x})} = \dfrac{\sqrt{x+1} - \sqrt{x}}{x+1-x} = \sqrt{x+1} - \sqrt{x}$.

83. **(E)**

As in the last problem, this expression requires that you recognize the difference of squares ($a^2 - b^2$). Here factor out the two expressions to get (999,999 +1)(999,999 -1) which is the same as (1,000,000)(1,000,000 -2). This can be rewritten as $(10^6)(10^6 - 2)$. Backsolving is also a very effective strategy here. Only choices (B) and (E) are the correct order of magnitude, and only choices (C) through (E) have the correct units digit, so (E) must be the answer.

84. **(D)**

It follows from $2x - 3b = 0$ that $b = \frac{2}{3}x$. So $b < 2$ implies $\frac{2}{3}x < 2$, or $x < 2(\frac{3}{2})$, which means $x < 3$. Since none of the other choices must be true (although $x > -3$ and $x < 2$ could be true), the answer is (D).

85. **(C)**

The maximum distance the fisherman could be from port would occur if he motors directly away from port on both occasions. This would put him $x = 15 + 3 + 6 = 24$ miles from port. The minimum distance he could be from port would occur if he followed fish directly back to port. This would put his distance from port at $x = 15 - (3 + 6) = 6$. So the fisherman must be between 6 and 24 miles from port, and the correct answer is (C).

86. **(D)**

(I.): When the absolute value of x is less than 1, raising it to a power >1 will produce a result with a smaller absolute value than x. For example $\left(\frac{1}{2}\right)^3 = \frac{1}{2} \cdot \frac{1}{2} \cdot \frac{1}{2} = \frac{1}{8}$ and $\frac{1}{8} < \frac{1}{2}$. However,

if x is negative then x^3 will still have a smaller absolute value than x, but it will have a larger actual value. For example $\left(-\frac{1}{2}\right)^3 = \left(-\frac{1}{2}\right)\left(-\frac{1}{2}\right)\left(-\frac{1}{2}\right) = \frac{1}{4}\left(-\frac{1}{2}\right) = -\frac{1}{8}$; and $-\frac{1}{8} > -\frac{1}{2}$; I is only true if $x > 0$, so we cannot say that it "must" be true. (II.): Similar to I, when the absolute value of x is less than 1, x raised to any power will have a smaller absolute value than x. Any number raised to an even power will yield an answer > 0, but less than the absolute value of x. For example, $\left(-\frac{1}{2}\right)2 = \frac{1}{4}$; So II must be true. (III.): By adding $x^5 + x^2$ to each side of this inequality, it can be rewritten as $x^4 + x^2 > x^3 + x^5$. First, we know from this that the left hand side of the equation must be positive (and the right hand side may be either positive or negative) due to the fact that any nonzero number raised to an even power must be positive, and anything raised to an odd power will have the same sign as the base. If x is negative, then statement III must be true. If x is positive, then it is a matter of determining whether the absolute value of the left side of (manipulated) equation is less than that of the right. When x is raised to higherpowers, the result becomes smaller and smaller the higher the power. So $x^2 > x^3$ and $x^4 > x^5$. Therefore III must be true. The correct answer is (D).

87. **(C)**

Clearly (1) alone and (2) alone are insufficient since there is a range of integers for which (1) is true and a range of integers for which (2) is true. Thus, the answer must be (C) or (E). To determine whether the two inequalities taken together, limit the range sufficiently to determine the value of x, one must solve each inequality. Inequality (1) is equivalent to $x > -4\frac{1}{2}$, and inequality (2) is equivalent to $x < -3$. If x is an integer and $-4\frac{1}{2} < x < -3$, then $x = -4$, and the answer is (C).

88. **(A)**

Most of the same algebraic methods used in equalities can be applied to the inequalities in the answer choices. Each answer choice must be individually evaluated to match the inequality in the question. For answer choice (A), first, subtract 3 from both sides.

$(-3) + (-5x) + 3 < 15 - 2x + (-3) \rightarrow -5x < 12 - 2x$

Next, add 2x to both sides of the inequality to isolate x.

$(+2x) + (-5x) < 12 - 2x + (+2x) \rightarrow -3x < 12$

Lastly, divide both sides by -3. However, in an inequality, when multiplying or dividing by a negative number, the direction of the inequality must be changed. For instance, in this example, the less than sign becomes greater than.

$\frac{-3x}{-3} < \frac{12}{3} \rightarrow x > -4$

Therefore, answer (A) is correct, and the other choices do not need to be attempted.

89. **(E)**

Because we know that m is negative or zero and n is positive, the product of the two must be a negative number or zero: $(-) \cdot (+) = (-)$. The only value of the five that mn cannot be is 19, which is positive. The correct answer is (E).

90. **(C)**

From (1) it can be determined that $x + 1 = 3$ or $x + 1 = 4$; thus $x = 2$ or $x = 3$. From (2) it can be determined that $x = 3$ or $x = 4$. Since the precise value of x cannot be determined from either (1) or (2) taken alone, the answer must be C or E. If (1) and (2) are considered together, the only value of x that satisfies both conditions is $x = 3$.

91. **(C)**

Statement (1) alone is not sufficient since $y > 7$ if $x < -3$ and $y = 7$ if- $3 < x < 4$. This can be found by trying a few values of x. Therefore, the answer must be (B), (C), or (E). Statement (2) alone is also not sufficient since $y > 7$ if $x > 4$. The answer must be (C) or (E). Taken together, statements (1) and (2) determine values of x for which $y = 7$. The answer is (C).

92. **(E)**

Clearly each statement alone is insufficient because we do not know anything about the value of x and therefore cannot make a judgment about y. By taking both pieces of

information and manipulating the inequalities, we can eliminate x. To combine them we need to have the inequality signs pointing in the same direction. This can be accomplished by multiplying the second inequality by -2. After that manipulation the second inequality looks like this: $-2x + 6y > -48$. Adding this inequality to the first eliminates x and gives the following result:

$2x + y > 27$

$-2x + 6y > -48$

$7y > -21$ so $y > -3$

From this we learn that y could be both negative or positive so the answer to the question is choice (E).

93. **(E)**

To answer the question definitively, you must know the signs of x and y. With each statement alone it is impossible to find any information on the signs of x an y. However, together, you can combine the two statements to find limits on x and y. Remembering the rules for inequalities, you must first manipulate the two inequalities so that the signs are pointing the same way. By multiplying the first inequality by -1, you get the following two inequalities which you can combine:

$-x + y < 5$

$x - 2y < -7$

$-y < -2$ or $y > 2$ Therefore, y must be positive.

Doing the same for x, you multiply the first inequality by -2 to get the following inequalities which you can combine:

$-2x + 2y < +10$

$x - 2y < -7$

$-x < 3$ or $x > -3$ Therefore x could be negative or positive.

As a result the product xy could be either positive or negative and the answer is (E).

94. **(D)**

1 ¤ z = -8 means that $(1 + 3)(z - 2) = -8$. Consolidating the terms in the left-most expression gives: $4(z - 2)=-8 \rightarrow z - 2 = -2 \rightarrow z = 0$; the correct answer is (D).

95. **(E)**

If $g(x) = \dfrac{x^4}{16}$ then $g(2x) = \dfrac{(2x)^4}{16} = \dfrac{16x^4}{16} = x^4$

In order to express $g(2x)$, which equals x^4, in terms of $g(x)$, which equals $\dfrac{x^4}{16}$, you must multiply $g(x)$ by 16. Therefore the answer is $16\,g(x)$.

96. **(D)**

This difficult question is testing the distributive properties of certain functions. If $g(c - d) = g(c) - g(d)$ then that means for some function listed in the answer choices this property is always true. For instance, $g(4 - 2)$ which is $g(2)$ must equal $g(4) - g(2)$, or $g(10-2)$ which is $g(8)$ must equal $g(10) - g(2)$. The numbers picked are arbitrary – they must only meet the condition given in the question. To see which answer is correct, either recognize the proper answer with your knowledge of distribution properties or plug in with some numbers (here using the example above) to see if $g(4 - 2)$ which is $g(2)$ will always equal $g(4) - g(2)$. By checking you see that this is only true for D where $g(2) = 10$ and $g(4) - g(2)$ also equals 10. It is not true for any of the other functions.